Cognitive Therapy & Dialectical Behavior Therapy for Anxiety -2 In 1-

Everything You Should Know About Treating Depression, Worry, Panic, PTSD, Phobias And Other Anxiety Symptoms With CBT & DBT

By

Jonathan Moran

Table of Contents

Cognitive Behavioral Therapy For Anxiety

Introduction 7

Chapter 1 Overview of CBT and why it works 10
    Pioneering Therapy... 10

Chapter 2 Understanding anxiety and the anxious mind
.... 20

Chapter 3 Developing your anxiety profile 29
    Matching Anxiety Types with Anxiety Programs....... 29

Chapter 4 Seven practical CBT skills to practice........... 41
    Improve condition and functioning to transform an anxious mind 41

Chapter 5 Exposure Therapy 88
    Anxious Fears.. 88
    Common Exposure Methods 91
    Does exposure therapy work? 93

Chapter 6 Formulating and executing a personalized plan.. 98
    Self Help Treatment for Anxiety Disorders 98

Chapter 7 How to move on and continue 106
    Maintaining a Healthy Outlook 108

Conclusion 112

References 114

Dialectical Behavior Therapy For Anxiety

Introduction 121

Anxiety: Understanding the Specifics 125
    What is it? 126
    Difference between Anxiety and Anxiety Disorders 131
    The Link between Anxiety and Avoidance 134
    Anxiety-related Problems 138
    Summary 140

Dialectical Behavior Therapy: An Overview 142
    What is DBT and How does it Work? 143
    Four Stages of DBT 147
    What makes DBT Different? 150
    DBT: A Recap 155
    Summary 156

DBT Distress Tolerance and Mindfulness Skills 158
    What are DBT Mindfulness Skills? 158
    The 'What' Skills 161
    The 'How' Skills 163
    DBT Mindfulness Skills- A Case Example 165
    What are DBT Distress Tolerance Skills? 167

Summary 173

DBT Interpersonal Effectiveness and Emotion Regulation Skills 175

What are DBT Interpersonal Effectiveness Skills? .. 181

Summary 187

Stress: The Basics 188

What Causes it? 188

Where does Stress Come from? 190

Using DBT to Manage Stress 193

Summary 195

Worry: Self-help Approaches 197

What Causes it? 197

Using DBT Skills to Manage Worry 199

Summary 205

Post-traumatic Stress Disorder: Recalling and Recovering 207

Identifying Post-Traumatic Stress Disorder 207

How does DBT help with Post-Traumatic Stress Symptoms 212

Summary 216

Panic Attacks: What it Feels Like? 217

What Causes Panic Attacks? 218

How do You Get Panic Attacks 218

Symptoms and Sequale 222

Summary 225
Social Anxiety: The Fear of People 227
    What Causes Social Anxiety? 228
    The Driving Factors 231
    The Role of Parenting Approaches and Styles 233
    Consequences of Social Anxiety 234
    Summary 236
Conclusion 237
Disclaimer 242

Cognitive Behavioral Therapy For Anxiety

How To Finally Break Free From Anxiety And Change Your Life Forever

By

Jonathan Moran

Introduction

Being anxious can seem like a small problem, we all feel it at some point in our lives. Whether it is speaking in public or sitting an exam, anxiety is a natural process. For some, anxiety can ruin their lives. Experiencing a panic attack is not a pleasant experience. It can be debilitating and restrict your day to day life.

Yet, the process of anxiety is a biological one. As the body enters emergency mode, a release of hormones rush at the brain, which reacts with a fight or flight response. Imagine if you felt like this all the time and not only when threatened! This is what happens to those who suffer from anxiety. Their body is constantly on edge, expecting danger.

You are reading this book for a reason. You may simply be curious, or you may want to learn more about the healing process from anxiety attacks. Help is at hand throughout these pages. It is important to understand what is happening to you as you face a draining panic attack. Only then can you begin to unravel the complexities of anxiety.

It is difficult to comprehend what a panic attack feels like unless you experience it firsthand. My own experiences cost me dearly. Gradually I withdrew from everyday life. I did anything to avoid that all too familiar feeling of dread. That's when my research began. Many years later I hold an MSc in Psychology, to substantiate my theories.

Now is the time to take back control of your inner self. To stave off future panic attacks, you should learn how your body reacts and how to take control. You can influence, to some extent, your hormonal release. This will stop those attacks right in their tracks. Amazingly, it is not a difficult task to take on. Once you do, your life will improve and you will gain the freedom to go anywhere at any time. It is liberating for those living under the sentence of anxiety.

Cognitive Behavior therapy (CBT) is a way of curing many mental health issues. It has a proven track record on conditions such as PTSD and GAD. For those reasons, CBT is one of the most widely used therapies for such conditions. There are various methods, all giving excellent results. Seeking professional help may entail individual or group therapy for 5-20 weeks in a clinic setting. Or you can look at self-help, using similar techniques.

By learning to identify the warning signals, you will learn to control future anxiety episodes. Simple relaxation exercises help you control the hormonal levels occurring in your body. CBT shows you how to change thought patterns so depression and panic are kept at bay.

When writing this book, it was my intention to show you how easy it is to change your life around. This is something you can begin today, not tomorrow or next week. Start the CBT sessions now! The sooner you start, the sooner you get your life back under control.

Do you suffer dark thoughts? CBT will help you change such thoughts around completely. Our inner emotions are the true grit of who we are. It stands to reason that if we connect with them we can balance our mental health processes.

Don't allow your self-esteem to plunge into the dark pits of insecurity, as your negative thinking takes over. Read on to find your secret inner powers, where CBT can help you lead a confident and normal life.

Chapter 1 Overview of CBT and why it works

Pioneering Therapy

Aaron Beck's pioneering work in psychotherapy led to the introduction of Cognitive Behavior therapy (CBT). He was an American Psychologist and professor at the University of Pennsylvania.

CBT has similarities to psychotherapy. Both relate to the treatment and possible cure for mental health conditions. CBT concentrates on thoughts, attitudes and beliefs and how these affect a person's behavior. It is based on the premise that how a person feels, acts and thinks, are all interconnected. If any one of these factors can be altered, then they can all be changed. This type of therapy targets the negative thought patterns that have led to the cycle of distorted behavior. It is a theory also known as Negative Reinforcement.

The understanding that thoughts can shape how a person feels and behave, is not a new concept. The Greek philosopher Epictetus said, *People are not disturbed by things, but by the view they take of them.* This is the basis of

CBT. It is not the situations that cause people to suffer mental health problems, but rather their own interpretation of them.

Therapists who work with CBT play more of a supervisory role, rather than a consultant. Their role is to oversee the client's personal development and ensure their wellbeing.

Emotional Reasoning

A major cause of mental health problems can be Emotional Reasoning. This refers to allowing emotions to determine thoughts.

> *For example, believing that something must be true because we feel it is.*

This can and does affect how people relate to the world.

> *For example, if you pass an acquaintance on the street and they do not respond to your greeting. Your reaction and thought pattern could be that you believe they do not like you.*

Though you don't know this for sure, but now you feel rejected. In turn, your thoughts further spiral into other negative aspects of yourself. If this was to happen on a regular basis, then your opinion of yourself is lowered. With low self-esteem comes depression and anxiety.

Cognitive Distortions

CBT attempts to challenge negative thought patterns. When they are identified, they will be replaced with positive thoughts. It attempts to identify common negative thinking styles, known as Cognitive Distortions, such as:

- Emotional Reasoning - I feel useless, therefore I am.
- Jumping to conclusions - That person ignored me today, they must dislike me.
- All or Nothing - Everything is Black and white, with no grey areas in-between. This can also be known as Labeling.
- Filtering - Giving prominence to your own failures rather than your successes. This is because the sufferer does not identify any successes.
- Overgeneralization - Thought patterns determine future outcomes.

> *For example, the failure to get a job after an interview could lead to Overgeneralization. The result of their experience distorts their thinking pattern, and they now believe that they will never get a job.*

These are only a few standards of Cognitive Distortions that can lead to mental health issues, such as depression and anxiety.

CBT attempts to tackle Cognitive Distortions by teaching the patient more positive ways of thinking. There are a few strategies to do this, but it usually begins with Functional Analysis. This means first identifying the negative thought patterns of the client. 'The therapist will then determine the behaviors that go with the Cognitive Distortion. With the goals in mind, the therapist will attempt to teach the patient new skills to overcome the negative thinking.

CBT is recognized as being useful for treating many mental health illnesses, such as:

- Depression
- Anxiety
- Addictions
- Phobias
- Eating disorders.

Text In the western world, the gold standard of counseling is seen as the best, defined by evidence in its success. CBT is one such therapy that falls into this status of "gold standard." Most patients suffering from mental health issues are referred for CBT treatment. It has many benefits over using medication as a treatment. As a stand-alone treatment, it also has fewer side effects than drugs. Often though, it can be combined with drug therapy.

How CBT therapy works

The primary goal of CBT is to tackle the negative thinking patterns that are the root cause of so many issues. It differs from other methods of psychoanalysis that tend to be more freestyle. They are often based on self-exploration, by using a set structure for their methods. There is still some self-exploration involved in CBT. Patients are encouraged to analyze their inner-feelings and more importantly, their deep thoughts. Sometimes the therapist may set homework for the patient to do alone. The following techniques can involve a worksheet for the patient to follow:

- Self-Journals - keeping a diary about their thoughts and emotions. Most especially when linked to events that may cause them problematic issues. This can be a good way to identify trigger points of certain emotions.

- Breaking down the Cognitive Distortions - seen as the main goal of CBT. Identifying harmful thoughts is the first step in learning how to control them.

- Cognitive rebalancing - this leads on to the next phase. Once the distortions are identified, it is then possible to find the root cause of those distortions. With help from a CBT counselor, the patient can then begin to understand why they feel the way they do. This is especially helpful if the patient's thoughts are harmful. It is an important step in helping them to challenge their thoughts.

- Interoceptive Exposure - also known as Gradual Exposure. A technique used to help treat panic attacks. Panic attacks often happen as a response to sensations in the body, such as shudders, tingling or even nausea. Interoceptive Exposure exposes the client to the feelings that bring on such sensations. The patient is guided to see that their thoughts are maladaptive or abnormal. They learn that i is the dysfunctional thinking that results in triggering a panic attack. They are encouraged to confront such thoughts and not avoid them. Only then can they recognize that the resulting sensations that come with the thoughts are not a threat. This method is also used to treat Obsessive Compulsive Disorder (OCD), and those who suffer from phobias.

- Progressive Muscle Relaxation - this uses relaxation exercises and is a similar technique to mindfulness. The exercises involve relaxing one muscle group at a time, until total relaxation of the body is achieved. Grossman et al (2004)(1a), carried out a meta-analysis of previous studies on this technique. He indicates that mindfulness can help with stress and anxiety. Breathing techniques are also used to help the patient achieve a state of relaxation.

- Functional Analysis - is a means of identifying the event that causes the cognitive distortions and behavior initially. In short, cause-effect-consequences. This method is usually accompanied by a worksheet. It allows the patient to make notes on the episode that causes the dysfunctional thoughts. They must record the behavior those thoughts instigated, and any consequences that followed.

There are a multitude of other techniques, or skills, which the supervisor can use in a CBT session. Far too many for the scope of this book. In understanding some of the techniques, it shows how this therapy can work.

Whilst there are many different skill sets in a CBT therapist's armory, there are also a few therapeutic approaches they can use.

- Cognitive Therapy - is the standard CBT approach. This method which looks at maladaptive/dysfunctional thoughts and how to change them

- Dialectical Behavioural Therapy (DBT) - an approach that was originally used to treat borderline personality disorder (BPD.) It was also found to be effective in treating a much wider range of issues. For Instance, eating disorders, substance abuse, bipolar, as well as many others.

- Multi-modal Therapy (MMD) - is an eclectic therapy that draws from other psychotherapies. MMD has a basis that there are seven different aspects to psychological functioning, known as the Basic ID. These are first assessed before treatment continues.

- Rational Emotive Behaviour Therapy (REBT) - an approach that can be used to help patients change irrational beliefs.

Does CBT Therapy work?

Among the non-pharmacutical remedies, CBT has the most clinical evidence to show its success. Studies show that it is at least as effective as using psychotropic drugs, for anxiety and depression and bipolar, Chang et al (2017) (1b).
Usually, CBT is a short-term treatment, often lasting for less than six months. Once the patient has developed new ways of thinking and how to challenge maladaptive thoughts, then over time they still benefit from CBT.

One reason this therapy is deemed effective is how the brain reacts to CBT. In an event such as an anxiety or a panic attack, certain areas of the brain are overreacting. These areas are known as the amygdala. It regulates emotions and the hippocampus which processes memory. Using brain scans on those who have anxiety issues, have shown that such brain regions return to normal levels of activity after CBT. Beutel et al (2010) (1c).

Chapter 2 Understanding anxiety and the anxious mind

Historical Treatment of Anxiety

The World Health Organization (WHO), reported that 300 million people worldwide suffer from depression. That is almost 1/5th of the world's population. Depression is also believed to be the No.1 contributing disability in the world. Anxiety disorders ranked at 6th. These statistics make sad reading. The US has one of the highest rates of anxiety. With 8 people in every 100, suffering anxiety disorders in some form WHO (2017).

Studies are also showing that common mental health disorders occur at a higher rate in the lower income sectors. Even more disturbing is the fact that anxiety disorders are treatable. Why then are the figures so high? Is it a modern epidemic?

In medieval times treatment consisted of blood leaches and bathing in freezing water. It was a real breakthrough when psychologists such as Sigmund Freud, started treating sufferers more as patients. Such patients began to undergo the "talking" therapy. It was not until as late as the 1980's that the American Psychiatric Association recognized "anxiety" as a mental health disorder. Before then, anxiety was simply classed as a "woman's problem." Sufferers became stigmatized and labeled as depressives. Women are twice as likely to suffer from anxiety disorders, but such conditions are by no means restricted to females only. Today, anxiety may be treated with medication as well as therapy.

What is Anxiety?

In days gone by, our ancestors risked their lives whenever they hunted live food. Luckily, these skills are no longer needed, but it brings us to how the body reacts when facing danger. This is a time when we instinctively make the decision of "fight, flight or freeze." It's not a choice brought on by conscious thought. Rather, it is set in motion by the release of chemicals in the part of our brain known as the limbic system. The chemical is cortisol, which is a steroid hormone released through the adrenalin glands. One of the side effects from raised levels of this hormone is anxiety. If you feel this type of anxiety too often, the high levels of cortisol can damage cells in a part of the brain known as the hippocampus. This is an area that helps process memories. Such damage can lead to impaired learning and loss of memory. McAuley et all (2009)(2a). de Quervain et al (1998) (2b).

Symptoms of Anxiety

Anxiety is now separated from the condition of depression. Although many who suffer from depression also have anxiety issues. Patients who suffer from depression tend to dwell on the past and feel very negative about themselves, and life in general. This is not typical in the case of patients suffering from anxiety. They will worry excessively about the here and now, or the future. Their lives are full of "what ifs," in the eventuality of a disaster. Symptoms of anxiety can vary in individuals, but here are a few to look out for:

- Feeling tense for no reason, on edge and almost nervous.
- The sense of dread and impending doom.
- Unable to sleep because of worry.
- General restlessness and fidgeting, unable to relax.
- Lack of concentration.
- Irritable for no reason.
- Breaking out in a cold sweat.
- Shaking.
- Feeling nauseous.
- Digestive and intestinal upsets.

Panic attacks can come as a result of feeling one or many of these symptoms. When someone has frequent anxiety attacks, it inevitably leads to ill health. This is because of the cortisol levels remain high too often and for too long. One of cortisol's roles is to increase blood sugars. Unbalanced and this can result in insulin resistance. In turn, this may lead to the late onset or type 2 diabetes. Hacket et al (2016) (2c).

In a modern fast-paced society with access to social media, many people are feeling more and more anxious about the world around us. This can start at an early age. If young people are not diagnosed and treated, their anxiety attacks will follow them into adulthood.

There are also various stages throughout life that can lead to feeling over anxious:

- Education

Learning and education should be an enjoyable experience. All too often children are pressured to meet certain academic targets. Those who don't meet them may very well consider themselves a failure. The burden of being successful lays heavy on the shoulders of young people.

- Family life.

This is a worrying time, particularly if you have never had responsibilities. Women are expected to raise families and go out to work at the same time. Such pressures create huge stresses in their daily lives. With the increasing break up of marriages, the pressure of anxiety reflects on both parents, and on the children.

- Materialism

People who live in wealthy industrialized countries are bombarded with a heavily commercialized culture. Advertising constantly prompts us to buy the newest and seemingly greatest ever products. Such deviant tactics imply that their goods will improve your life and make you happy. It seems we must keep up with all the latest gadgets to have an attractive home, and wear the latest fashion labels to look good. All increasing the pressures of life as we attempt to earn more money to keep up.

- The Anxious Mind

Whilst it might seem to be stating the obvious, worry plays a key role in anxiety. People who suffer from anxiety attacks are likely big worriers. Often, the only way a worrier will stop panicking over a specific problem is if they have moved on to a different one. Worry leads to anxiety until the released chemicals mean the person cannot think rationally. At this point, they will jump to conclusions of their own making. Unable to focus on reality because their minds are highly aroused, the problem is no longer solvable. They cannot see any solutions which then leads deeper into anxiety.

- Simple Coping Techniques

For those who experience the build-up of burdening pressures and suffer anxiety attacks, there is help available. We will look at this in more detail later in this book. There are lifestyle changes that can be put into practice, using techniques to nip the anxiety attacks in the bud. A sufferer may find that these techniques are all they need to alleviate the experience of anxiety. Such as:

- Discussing your anxiety issues with your doctor. Doctors can prescribe medication to help you initially, and then refer you to a CBT therapist.

- Look at the foods you eat and what you drink. Caffeine and alcohol can both effect anxiety levels negatively. Take the general advice and at the very least cut down on the intake of foods known to cause such effects.

- Exercise is beneficial, but it doesn't mean you must work-out like crazy at a gym. Go on walks in calm and soothing vistas, if possible. Learn relaxation exercises that you can do sitting at a desk or watching TV, such breathing exercises and muscle relaxation.

- Try and keep active so you tire yourself out naturally during the day. That way sleep will come easier at night.

Stress and anxiety are closely related conditions. Though it is possible to suffer one without suffering the other. For both, you should seek help but there are many self-help techniques that you can do to ease some of the immediate pressures.

Anxiety can include phobias and is often only triggered in certain circumstances. Stress is more a build-up of worry because there is too much pressure in your life. Something has to give. We will look at ways of helping yourself to cope with anxiety. Many of the coping methods are ways to ease the pressures, are similar to the stress self-help approach. It could be that stress is what has brought on your anxiety in the first place. Deal with one and the other may ease as well.

Recognizing that you are suffering from anxiety is the first stage. Events such as employment interviews will naturally cause anxious feelings, these are normal. You should not worry about anxiety when associated with common stressful events. Having adrenalin coursing through your system when under such stress, is a way your body copes with the situation. When you come out of the interview, the anxiety should lift to be replaced with relief that the stress is over. Of course, you may then stress while you wait for the results but try not to be over anxious in such situations.

It is when you are anxious over too many things, especially every day and maybe even all day. This is unhealthy as you will be producing those hormones we mentioned earlier, in high amounts. If you find that stress is affecting your everyday life, then it is time to seek help. The stress will mount up causing triggers to anxiety attacks. Hopefully, you will recognize the dire situation before it gets to that point.

If you have suffered anxiety attacks for over 6 months, this is known as Generalized Anxiety Disorder (GAD). Our next chapter will help you to assess yourself and recognize if this is you.

Chapter 3 Developing your anxiety profile

Matching Anxiety Types with Anxiety Programs

> *Quote: Natalie Goldberg Author who believes in and explores Zen Buddhism. "Stress is an ignorant state. It believes that everything is an emergency."*

Self-diagnosis is not encouraged when it comes to health issues, but anxiety can be eased with self-control. To do this, you will need to think about "when, where and what" triggers your own symptoms. Because there are various types of anxiety, it could be helpful to recognize which one you are suffering from. Learning the various types of anxiety and seeking the correct treatment for it, is important in the process of self-help. We will go into detailed treatment options later in this book. This chapter will look at ways you can identify your anxiety type and outline possible options for self-help treatment.

Let's start with some of the more serious profiles for the onset of anxiety. Post-Traumatic Stress Disorder (PTSD) is not as prevalent as generalized anxiety. The rarer types are usually brought on from specific events. By learning the various anxiety types, it will help you categorize your own anxiety profile. Once you understand your own profile, you will be better able to know which treatments might help you.

PTSD

Situation:

This relates to people who have experienced a traumatic incident that is out of the ordinary. It is usually an event that is not considered the norm, such as:

- Soldiers in combat.
- Childhood abuse.
- Rape or physical attack.
- Witnessing a murder.
- Natural disasters.

This list is only an example, but it shows the unusual circumstances that someone suffering PTSD may have gone through.

Symptoms:

They will suffer symptoms such as:

- Reliving the experience as if in a daydream. The event will play out in their minds with a feeling that the experience is happening right here and now.
- Reliving the experience in a nightmare when they sleep.
- Bad dreams will lead to broken sleep.
- Broken sleepwalk lead to irritability.
- Trigger points can set off the memory and lead to a panic attack.
- They may begin to avoid places and people. This is because they become frightened of any reminders of the traumatic event.
- Anger issues can set in as they are always on guard.
- Sufferers may become easily startled and have difficulties concentrating.

PTSD sufferers may find their minds focusing on the traumatic memories more and more each day. This can lead to the inability to cope with the normality around them. Sadly, they may try to forget by taking drugs or alcohol.

The onset of PTSD symptoms can be delayed by months or

even years after their experiences. It can be a gradual process before the patient finally breaks down. Anxiety symptoms may not be diagnosed until it comes in the form of panic attacks. It is likely that they will suffer the symptoms of depression first. PTSD does not only effect victims of traumatic incidents, it can include anyone who witnesses such an event.

Treatment:

Self-help alone cannot treat the symptoms someone with PTSD will suffer. Only when a PTSD patient can control their maladaptive thought process, can they begin their self-help process

- Medication can be an important first step and a valuable tool in the beginning of their treatment.
- Attending group sessions with other PTSD suffers can help them to talk about their experiences. Support groups will consist of fellow sufferers, so the patient can see that they are not alone.
- Family counseling can be helpful to allow those closest to them to understand what they are going through. This also helps families to realize their loved one is suffering an illness. Then they too can provide that all important support.

Phobias

This is when a person feels afraid of a particular sight, smell or situation.

Situation:

- It could come in the form of seeing insects, blood or even certain smells.
- Or it could come from an experience of heights or being enclosed in an elevator.

Symptoms:

- When in that situation, they begin to imagine extreme consequences; What if I fall and die and nobody finds me? What if the spiders go inside my body? What if the elevator gets stuck and no one knows?
- Feelings will be a sense of dread, shallow breathing, dizziness, cold sweats, nausea.
- It can bring on a panic attack.
- They will begin to avoid any situation that might entail such fears. Someone with a fear of spiders may no longer enjoy working in a garden, even though they loved to before their phobia took hold.

Treatment:

- It may be a combination of self-help exercises similar to stopping a panic attack.
- Plus, there will be an element of exposure therapy which we cover in another chapter.

OCD

Situation:

- Someone suffering from OCD may have spent many years with generalized stress and anxiety.
- They may have suffered a terrible experience that brought on their anxieties in the first instance.
- It could be a build-up of many situations as to why an OCD sufferer becomes obsessed.

Symptoms:

- Everything around them is exaggerated and distressing in their minds.
- They feel that the world around them is intruding upon them all the time. To overcome this, they may pray over and over or repeat certain words of comfort to themselves.
- Other forms of OCD can lead to obsessive cleanliness and everything must be orderly.

- One OCD symptom is that of hoarding, in case they need it later.
- They will probably be aware of their irrational behavior, but cannot stop.
- Some have intrusive and disturbing thoughts. Thoughts such as, if I don't spin around to the left 3 times, then someone in my family might come to harm. Or they may imagine they will get a disease if their home is not clean and tidy.
- For some, everything must be placed in a particular order.
- For others, they must carry out their rituals in a certain order.
- OCD is how they relieve their anxieties.

When it takes an extended time to complete rituals, it can take over their lives and become debilitating.

Treatment:
- Medication may be an option.
- Support from family members will be encouraged.
- Group therapy means sharing their worries and admitting their obsessive behavior.

- Exposure therapy is a good option for those who avoid certain situations. Learning to confront their fear and seeing that all is still well in the world.

As with most anxiety conditions, it is all about gaining control again.

Panic Attacks

Situation:

This type of profile is more one of sudden intense fear.

- A sufferer may, or may not, know the reason for the reason for the onset of sheer fear.
- It is almost always a reaction to a bodily sensation, such as increased heartbeat or tightness in the chest.
- Symptoms:
- Heavy and fast breathing.
- This can lead on to a tingling sensation.
- Dry mouth causing and you may have difficulty swallowing, or even feel like they are choking.
- Hot and cold sweats.
- Light headedness and dizziness, believing they might collapse.

- Impending doom that something bad is about to happen.
- Imagining terrible scenarios, such as:
  - "I'm going to die."
  - "Someone is going to attack me, I don't feel safe."
  - "There's going to be a disaster and I won't be able to get away.
  - "I've lost all control."

The sufferer has started to feel anxious for some reason, and it has led on to a full-blown panic attack.

For example: You are sat in your car on the freeway in a huge traffic jam. Normally you're patient in such situations, but you have a meeting to get to. Already the stress is setting in because you have no control over the situation. Then, you hear a car backfire and it triggers off an anxious thought. You start thinking, "What if someone's running lose with a gun and we all think it's just a car backfiring?" Now you won't get out of the car because you're imagining bad things. This makes you feel trapped so your anxious thoughts take control of you. You can't breathe and you're all alone in the car. You start to imagine that you're going to have a heart attack. You start to breath quick and shallow breaths, which leads onto a tingling in your fingers. That's it, now you know that today you are going to die. All the signs are right. You are now in a full-blown panic attack.

Can you see how this happened?

- Clearly, this person is already suffering stress.
- They must get to the important meeting on time.
- Frustration is setting in as the delay increases their stress levels.
- This could play out in many ways. Perhaps, in the same scenario, the driver gets out of the vehicle and starts shouting and swearing at no one in particular. Then, if someone responds, the driver abuses them as they have now become the focus of their target.

The entire scenario has been caused by stress.

- Do you recognize any of these feelings happening to you, whereby you blow a situation out of proportion?

- See how easy stress can lead to feeling anxious, which can bring on a full-blown panic attack?

Treatment:

- Self-help treatment will be learning how to recognize and deal with the symptoms before they blow out of proportion.
- It may also involve medication initially, to help with relaxation.
- Learning simple relaxation exercises, such as mindfulness and deep breathing.

Generalized Anxiety

Situation:

We have looked at many anxiety conditions. Yet, being over-anxious can happen to anyone who is overloaded with stress. The main problem with generalized anxiety is that it never goes away. Everyone has everyday worries to contend with.

Symptoms:

- The first signs you are not coping is when you are constantly worrying until the worry is on your mind all the time.
- It will be a build-up to lots of small worries, such as will you get somewhere on time? Who's doing the school run? How can you pay bills?
- You may find yourself not eating breakfast because you woke up worrying.
- Suffering constipation because your body is to tense.
- Constant headaches.
- The situation escalates until you feel physically ill.

Treatment:

- Recognize that you are suffering anxiety.
- Self-help treatment begins with mindfulness. Recognizing; Acceptance; Setting out a plan of action to ease the stresses in your daily life.

Chapter 4 Seven practical CBT skills to practice

Improve condition and functioning to transform an anxious mind

The cycle of an anxiety attack is based on a trigger, usually a physical sensation, that leads to negative thoughts. Our imagination then runs wild. A roller coaster of mixed emotions result in our response and behavior. Yet, we as individuals with agency can learn to exert some control over this process. Self-help is an excellent option for the pathway of eliminating anxiety. As with any self-motivational task, practice leads to greater control.

There are many approaches to CBT therapy. Let's look at seven of them, to see how different CBT therapeutic methods can heal an anxious mind.

1. Journals and Data Gathering

When you are suffering from a constant barrage of negative thoughts, it can be a very disturbing experience. It is not always easy to control the thoughts in your head. Particularly so when you are on a downward spiral of emotions. This is a time when need to learn exactly who your inner self really is.

Inner mind-talk

Do you ever talk to yourself? We can do this silently in our minds, or even out loud if you feel comfortable enough to do so. Don't worry or feel embarrassed, we all do it. It is when you do not realize that you are talking to yourself that it may become a mental health concern. If you catch yourself doing it, then you know all's well. Your inner self is attempting to organize and take control. Studies have shown that it is good to converse with yourself. One study indicates that when we talk out loud to ourselves, it actually boosts concentration. This, in turn, helps us to achieve our goals with the task in hand. (Kirkham, Breeze & Mari-Beffa (2011) (4.1a)

As you worry over a problem, your mind is gathering information to think up solutions. It could be described as data gathering if we were computers. As we're human though, it can be very distracting when your mind will not shut down.

Sometimes our mind-talk can be unhelpful. Especially if the thoughts are negative, and/or coming at us at inappropriate times. It can drive you to distraction. For instance at 2 am in the morning when you keep telling yourself to "go to sleep," and all your mind wants to do is worry. Later we will discuss breathing techniques for such relaxation. If this fails then don't lay there suffering, get up and read a book, listen to music, go get a drink of water. Any activity that may help to redirect your inner thoughts away from the constant state of worry.

You need to learn to deal with those worrying thoughts in a different way. Stop your mind from running away with inner thoughts at inappropriate times. There is a technique that will identify negative thoughts that keep re-occurring in your mind and redirect them. You will be digging into the mental noise that you may not even be aware of. You will achieve this by creating a journal of things that happen to you. In this journal, you will be encouraged to record the event and your feelings at the time. Later you will study the recordings and find solutions.

For example:

John is rushing to catch a bus to return home after his working day. It's the bus he gets at the same time every day. As he approaches the bus stop he can see who is waiting, and he stops rushing. He begins to think that maybe he'll let the bus go and catch the next one, even though it hasn't even arrived yet. Why is he suddenly afraid of catching a bus that he had been rushing to get?

It is not being on a bus that he is anxieties about. It is the people at the bus stop. They are fellow work colleagues and they are sat chatting and laughing. He's panicking as he is not a very popular person. He wonders should he talk to them and risk them ignoring him? Or should he ignore them and risk them thinking him unsocial? His mind is ticking over fast. Every thought becomes more negative, even to the point that he decides to go home using a different route. Only moments before he was in a good mood looking forward to catching the bus to get home. Now he wants to avoid the bus altogether and he'll get home later.

The result could be that John will have to go out of his way to go home a different way. This may lead on to other problems such as leaving work later, when his work colleagues have gone. John has resolved nothing, only made his life harder.

In reality, all he needed to do was smile at one person in the group and respond if necessary. Instead, one negative thought led to another and the whole situation became unbearable for him.

Let's suppose that when John gets home, he writes the incident down in a journal. He would be encouraged to dissect the situation more slowly. It is an opportunity to review every thought and feeling he had in those speedy moments of panic. It is a way at pulling out your inner thoughts. Asking yourself questions about what you have written. Looking at other ways of how you "could" have dealt with the situation. This is a proven way of taking your time to assess what you perceived to be an anxious situation.

Writing a daily journal of your movements and feelings to study later, will give you an idea of your triggers. Use headings, such as "event," "emotion," "notes." You don't need to write down everything you do in a day, only the stressful situations.

What you need to do is focus on recording any flashes of anxiety, as John did in the example. Later that day, you can read what you were thinking at the time, pulling out on important key points. When John reads his diary log about his experience at the bus stop, he may see that it would not have been that difficult to get his usual bus. By seeing the truth of the situation, he will not change his route home. Instead, he will simply smile at those he knows. That is enough social grace to acknowledge their presence without too much input from him. If they don't respond, then at least he has not made a fool of himself. Already he has achieved a goal; confronting people he doesn't feel comfortable with and refusing to go home a different way.

Worksheet Ideas

Daily Activity Diary

- This is about logging your activity during the day. At the end of the week, or in a therapy session, you then reflect upon your diary to help you evaluate your thoughts and actions.
- Workload It's not necessary to complete every session, every day if very little is happening.

- Activity. These are actives that brought about emotional responses. You don't need to write about the mundane tasks, such as cleaning your home. It is more important to focus on events that may cause you anxiety or fluctuations in your mood swing.
- Thoughts. When you write something in the Activity section, then you need to fill in the rest of the columns. In this section, it's so you know whether your thoughts were negative or not.
- Mood. Here you should grade your mood between 1-10 at the time of the event. When you study the diary later, it will show you what makes you panic and what makes you moody.
- Answer problems. Try to think of ways to deal with the events that you are logging. Look at what you went wrong and write how you could have stopped it, or done things differently. You can put these answers in at the end of the day, or the end of the week when you come to studying your diary. if you do it later

then you will not feel as emotional as when the event happened.
- **Replacement Statement.** This part is about counteracting any negative thoughts you had during the day. Pick out the parts of your day where you achieved something, no matter how trivial. Write about your day in a positive light.

Time	Activity	Thoughts	Mood 1= Great 10= Depressed	Answer to any problems
6 – 8 am	*Stayed in bed*	*Don't want to get the train to work.*	*8-Tired*	*Should get up earlier.*
8 - 10 am	*Missed Brkfst, in a rush.*	*Caused myself to get stressed. Hate rushing*	*9-Panic I'll be late to work.*	*Set 2 alarms to get up earlier.*
10am – 12noon	*Ate unhealthy lunch as hungry.*	*Hate my job*	*7-Dreading journey home.*	*Get a job nearer home.*

12 - 2pm	*Supervisor gave me a telling off as I did some wrong inputting.*	*She's always had it in for me!*	*10-Angry.*	*I should get a new job.*
2 - 4pm		*I know it was my fault not my supervisors.*	*5*	*Stop worrying about journey home.*
4 - 6pm	*Train packed.*	*Should I sit here and wait for crowd to go.*	*10-Panickin!*	*I must stop doing that journey.*
6 - 8pm	*Finally got home.*	*Relieved to be home. I hate my life!*	*10-Crying.*	*Need to buy a car.*
8 - 10pm	*Go to bed early.*	*I like my job really. It's just the journey.*	*6-Fed up.*	*Save up for a car.*
10pm – 12mdnt	*Asleep for 10*			

> Replacement Statement: *Today I went to work even though I didn't want to go. I got on a train with lots of people which means that I am a brave person. My boss told me off but I deserved it as I did something wrong. I need a car but can't afford one, Instead, I'm going to be an early riser. I will defeat this problem by getting an earlier train that isn't so busy.*

Add new columns that are relevant to your own personal situation, if you wish to add more detail.

Note that the replacement statement is for you to change around the negative aspects of your day. Remind yourself of what you have achieved. In our example the client DID get to work, despite sleeping in. They DID get on the busy train, despite hating crowds. They DID take the criticism from their boss and admitted it was their own fault.

The idea behind these worksheets is for you and your therapist to study how you're behaving and thinking during a normal week. Then to analyze it and find solutions to many issues.

2. Cognitive Restructuring

This type of therapy is fundamental to CBT. It is also known as Cognitive Reframing. The idea behind it is to analyze negative thoughts and give them a whole new meaning. In this way, you are challenging those maladaptive thoughts.

Stress-producing thoughts are called Cognitive Distortions. Such a negative mindset affects your inner mood, making you unhappy and causing anxiety. With Cognitive Reframing the goal is to challenge Cognitive Distortions. To do this you will replace them with more positive cognitions and so reduce stress.

When a negative thought occurs due to a trigger, it can send you on a downward spiral of depression. This increases stress levels and ruins the quality of your life. Once in a negative mood swing, performance is affected. and you will find yourself becoming anxious at the most innocuous of situations. If you can learn to turn this around, then you will have much better control of your inner thoughts.

The process of Cognitive Restructuring was developed in the 1950's by psychologist, Albert Ellis. It was part of his development of Rational Emotive Behavior Therapy (REBT).

It is successful in helping to treat many nervous disorders. Bryant et al (2006) carried out a study of this for PTSD sufferers(4.2a). The results indicated that Cognitive Restructuring was effective in reducing depression and maladaptive thinking in PTSD patients. It is not only anxiety issues that Cognitive Restructuring can play a positive role. Boelen et al (2007), showed that Cognitive Restructuring combined with Exposure Therapy, successfully helped in bereavement interventions (4.2b). This approach helped to reduce the effects of grief

The capacity to store memories is an amazing function. It helps to guide us safely through our lives. We refer to past-experiences when making choices and decisions. Through those memories, we make assumptions about what will happen in any given situation. If we have had a bad experience, that memory will fixate itself into our minds. Difficulties can then arise when faced with the same or similar situation. As our anxiety increases because of a bad memory, we tend to blow the memory out of all proportion. This can escalate into a downward spiral of anxiety. Let's suppose that the past-experience is analyzed through Cognitive Restructuring. When confronting a similar situation in the future, you will approach it more positively.

The intent is to identify the negative thoughts and challenge them. By modifying the irrationality that you have given them, you will start to realize the truth of your negative assessment. Remember that how you think affects how you feel. By turning that thought into a good one, it will improve your overall wellbeing.

For example. You are standing in a remote train station waiting for a train. You are feeling alone and vulnerable. Your heart is racing and you begin to feel afraid, even though there are no actual signs of danger. This, in turn, sets off negative thoughts, such as, "What if someone attacks me?" Once this thought takes a grip, it can be difficult to shake the feeling of peril. Now you are feeling anxious.

If you can learn to recognize when this happens, you will have the control to realize that your thoughts are irrational.

Only then can you try to turn those negative cognitions into positive ones. Force yourself to think positively regarding your situation. Look at the good in the situation, such as, "This place is surrounded by nature and it's beautiful." "Sitting here waiting is so peaceful and relaxing."

Already your mind is healing as you replace the maladaptive thoughts with positive ones. To help in this process you could try using a relaxing technique, such as the breathing exercise. If you are successful, it will help if you are ever in a similar situation again. Instead of it inducing anxiety, you will seek the positives in your situation and take strength from them. If you're memories of remain negative, you may inadvertently take the route of avoidance and never visit that station again. As we have already discussed, avoidance only helps to reinforce Cognitive Distortions. Even if nothing bad ever happened in that place, you convince yourself that you are going to be the first victim. You magnify the whole experience and turn it into a negative situation.

There are many techniques used by Cognitive Restructuring. All ways of helping you challenge a bad situation.

Decatastrophizing

Also known as the 'What if' technique. This method uses mental imagery. It is used on patients suffering from Cognitive Distortions. They will be encouraged to think about the most severe outcome of the situation or object that has caused their anxiety. This helps to determine if the patient has over exaggerated the threat. At the same time, it will show them if they have underestimated their ability to cope.

Thought Awareness

This method targets being aware of the Cognitive Distortions that cause the anxiety. By pulling out the memories mentally, it helps to understand how and why they cause maladaptive thinking. It can be difficult, especially if when in the middle of a panic attack. Trying to unpick the thought processes that brought on the anxiety is a mentally painful process. It is useful for determining triggers that bring on the feelings of unease and panic.

Socratic Questioning

This is using a set routine for questioning maladaptive thoughts. It's named after the Greek Philosopher, Socrates. He argued that through systematic questioning we can understand and deconstruct ideas. In turn, this will either verify those ideas or dismiss them. With Socratic questioning, it is necessary to first identify the Cognitive Distortions. With logical questioning, it will either lend clarification to the patient's theory or challenge it.

Thoughts appear as dialogue in our minds, along with a few visual images. A trained therapist will encourage patients to share negative thoughts. Then, they will ask questions that might challenge such thoughts.

Typical self-questions could be:

- Are the thoughts you are having based on feelings or facts? What evidence do you have that verify your opinion?

- Is there an alternative explanation of how you are seeing a situation? If there is, how would that change the way you now feel?

- What are the consequences of the situations you perceive, and what is the best or worst case outcome? How will you cope with those outcomes?

- Will other people have the same answers to that thought as you do? If not, why would they come to different conclusions?

- Are you looking at only the black and white areas, and not seeking the grey parts?

-

There are no correct answers to such questions. It is a means of unraveling maladaptive thinking. This sort of session should help the patient to analyze their negative thoughts. Helping to bring out the reasons why they think them. Then helping to defuse such thoughts.

This method also shows the patient how to question their own irrational fears. Socrates questioning does not necessarily need two people. Once the patient has been shown how to question themselves, they can use it on their own negative thoughts.

3. Behavioral Experiments

We have discussed the benefits of altering thoughts in helping to control anxiety. Now we will move on to behavioral experiments, which involves acting out thoughts. This process helps to reinforce the positives from the thought exercise. It is about re-enacting the negative thoughts in a real situation to study the outcome.

When an anxious person asks themselves "what if," it can start a spiral of anxiety. behavioral experiments on thought exercises can help them see that the outcome may not be as bad as they expected. By using behavioral experiments, the patient can act out that "what if" scenario to see that the result may, in fact, be a positive one.

It is a way of testing out the hypothesis raised by the patient on the imaginary "what if" situation. This is a common therapy for CBT and there are variations to carry out the experiments. It is about testing for and against a worrisome anxious situation, by role-playing the different scenarios.

To begin with, it should start with the help of the therapist, or even in group therapy session. It can also involve going out into a public setting to enact the theory. At the same time, the patient will have a worksheet to record their emotions, feelings, and thoughts both before and after the experiment. This is to reflect upon later, so the patient can see the exact outcome of their imagined anxiety.

It is not only about analyzing the outcomes, but it is also about learning coping strategies. Through the role-play method, the patient is encouraged to cope with situations they find difficult.

Let's use an example to play this out:

> Jenny hates going to the store. It is gradually got worse when the store was busy. To start with, she would try to go on quiet days. But she began to imagine everyone was watching her, or the store staff looked at her as though she was going to steal something. It became so difficult for Jenny that she slowly stopped going to any stores.
>
> The behavior exercise could begin in a group

session, with people she knows acting as the customers. She could think up situations that worry her, such as a customer staring at her. Between herself, her therapist and the others in the group, they could decide how she could approach the person looking at her, in a calm way. Perhaps she could smile at them and say "hi," but the thought of doing this scares her. If she can manage to do it in the group, eventually she may be able to do it in the store. Later in the program, her therapist will take her to a small store. The group members may join them and enact the scenario out in public. This way, Jenny gets to do her role-playing in a public setting.

What can Jenny learn through her behavioral experiment?

- Jenny will be encouraged to write notes about her feelings and anxiety levels.
- This is a controlled way to confront those dreaded "what ifs?"
- Building up confidence through role play.
- Practicing assertion.

- Learning how to approach and talk to a stranger in a calm manner.
- More importantly, Jenny is learning coping mechanisms for situations that she fears. If it does happen and some stranger stares at her when she is alone, she will now know how to deal with it without embarrassing herself.

By exposing Jenny to her dreaded thoughts, it has shown her that even if the worse was to happen, she can still cope with it. It is a form of exposure treatment, but it is also so much more. Jenny could practice eye contact during group sessions to help build up confidence in approaching other people. In their role play as customers, the others in the group can put her on the spot. They could ask her which row the bread is on. She would need to create an image in her head of a shop and put herself visually in the rows to create an answer. All helping to put her in a situation she has not been able to cope with.

It is a way of building up a picture of something the patient dreads, and then confronts it. All the while, the patient is supported and encouraged.

Of course, it cannot cover life-threatening situations. It is more for dealing with social anxiety, such as asking for directions, eating in public, or going in an escalator. All such fears that can be overcome with behavioral exercises.

Successive Approximation

It also lends the patient another coping mechanism of Successive Approximation. They are learning to break a huge problem into smaller pieces. Each step of the way will get harder and they cannot move forward until they have successfully achieved the previous step. The reward is a mental one; they can move on to the next stage until they achieve their final goal. What better reward is there than that. It shows the patient that if they continue to practice breaking down problems in a similar fashion, such as note taking and analysing those notes to move on, they can find a way to tackle their anxieties as they happen.

Worksheet Ideas

This is a way of encouraging and recording a patient's feelings of dread. It is in the form of an experiment that is first rehearsed in role play. Sometimes it may end there, or it may go on to be carried out in public, but in a controlled setting.

Taking the example we used in the chapter, here's what type of questions could go onto this experiment log sheet.

Q. What is the Fear?

A. Unable to go into stores for fear of being judged.

Q. What do you think will happen in the stores?

A. People stare at me and shop assistants look at me suspiciously like I'm a shoplifter.

Q. How do you see Design of the Experiment playing out.

A.
- Roleplay in group sessions to include other customer reactions in a store.
- Followed by role-play in a public setting, to include other members of the group and the therapist.

The log sheet should be designed around the individual experiment. The client can then record each session, logging their feelings as the dreaded situation plays out. In the case study, we have suggested it could be as follows:

Session 1:

Q. What is the role play?

A, Group members play customers. One will ask me where an item is in the imaginary shop. We have agreed beforehand to base it on a local store that we know. I am to describe where the item is. I will visually imagine myself standing by the main entrance. Then I will explain to the customer how to get to the right row.

Q. What are your feelings Before, During and After the experiment?

A.

- Before: I felt embarrassed at the role play.
- During: I had heart palpitations and difficulty breathing because I was thinking about being in the store.
- After: I felt more confident because the "customer" smiled at me and thanked me. It went well thanks to my group.

Session 2:

Q. What was the role play?

A group member played a shopper who stared at me as I walked around tables that represented store shelves. I had set questions that were considered as the "norm, that myself and the group agreed upon. I approached the group member "shopper," with these questions to help me deal with talking to her.

Q. What were your feelings Before, During and After the experiment?

A.

- Before: I was uncomfortable as the group member watched me walking around the tables. I had been encouraged to visualize myself in the store and that's what unbalanced me.
- During: In the past, I would have left the store. This time I asked the set questions that I would not have thought up by myself. They were comfortable questions, such as, "you look familiar, do we know each other?" It forced the other person to speak to me, which I was dreading. The aim was to ask a question that is friendly and maybe force a friendly

reaction. I was okay in the role play but not sure I can follow this through in a real life.
- After: I like the idea of thinking up friendly questions. If someone stares at me, I might dare myself to ask them where to find something. That way I can see if they act strangely towards me.

Session 3:

Q. What was the role play?

A. Those involved in my group went with me to a small store. We enacted the role-play that we'd done in the sessions.

Q. What were your feelings Before the experiment, During and After?

We can't give real answers and results to this experiment, as it is imaginary. The purpose is to give you an idea of how to go about a behavioral experiment. It is all about role-playing out those dreaded "what ifs," rather than just thinking about them. The group therapy should always be supervised by a professional therapist to achieve the best results. It is meant to guide the client towards possible ways to overcome the reasons for their anxiety.

4. Pleasant Activity Scheduling (AS)

This technique is a type of Behavioral treatment but does not involve role-playing. It is more about the patient influencing their own Behavioral Activation System (BAS)
.

The BAS is part of a hypothesis advocated in 1970, by British Psychologist Jeffrey Gray. Based on physiological responses, it is known as the Biopsychological Theory of Personality. Today, it is a widely-accepted conjecture within the psychological disciplines.

There are two main facets to this motivational neural model. One is the Behavioral Inhibition System (BIS), and the other is BAS. Each system is activated by different situations.

- The BIS leads to the negative stimuli of punishment and avoidance.
- The BAS leads to more positive stimuli, such as motivation and rewards.

Gray argued that BIS is the initial cause of anxiety.

Pleasant Activity Scheduling (AS) is primarily used for depression. It can also have benefits for those who suffer from the symptoms of anxiety. A study by Chu, et al (2009), indicates that students suffering from anxiety and or depression, received clinical benefits from BAS (4.4a). Using "AS" as a treatment for anxiety involves planning engaging activities. By doing so, it will result in the patient having positive experiences to look forward to. In a sense, patients are rewarding themselves. This is particularly useful for PTSD sufferers.

AS discourages isolation. It is aimed at getting patients to engage in positive activities to keep their minds active in a constructive way. Tailoring the events around the anxiety issues is an effective part of the course. For instance, if you are nervous about the sea, don't go on a boat trip. Unlike Exposure Therapy where you would need to face your fears, this is more about seeking pleasure to result in positive thinking. Even the planning can be an exciting part of the experience. Sometimes the build-up to an event can invoke happiness. The patient will be thinking about what they are looking forward to. This creates a better means of inner reflection to the normal negative anxious irrationalities.

By increasing activity levels, there is less opportunity to

brood over negative thoughts. The planning and the taking part in PA, are all distracting the thought process away from maladaptive thinking. Instead, it forces the patient to focus on positive and happier contemplations. AS should be taken at a pace the patient is comfortable with, and not rushed. Whether it includes only one activity planned in a week, or several activities, is not the key issue. In fact, it is better not to over plan, risking the possibility of panic. The point is to pull away from the normal environment and experience a feel-good factor

> *For instance, if you are stuck in your home most of the time, then imagine the great sense of achievement at getting to go out and about. Particularly so if you end up enjoying it.*

For a patient suffering from depression, this therapy would be aimed at making them feel more motivated. It should serve to increase their energy drive and push them forward. For anxiety though, it is more used as a distraction. It works by pulling the patient away from their daily negative thinking patterns, that they are so often trapped within.

It is not for everyone. For some, it may not be an easy type of exercise, though it is not done alone. A therapist will instruct a patient on how best to go about AS, though there will be many exercises encouraged as homework.

When choosing activities, it is good to choose healthy ones, here are a few suggestions. They won't suit everyone so feel free to add your own:

- Going out in the evening with a friend, maybe to the movies.
- Booking a sauna or message, a great way to help relax your body.
- Swimming, or joining an exercise class such as yoga.
- Going out for a "nature day" such as bird watching or strolling around a forest or lake.
- Booking a sports session such as badminton or tennis with a friend at a gym, or playing basketball.
- Going to a beach for the day.
- Joining a local group, ie book or gardening club.

If you don't feel ready to go out and plan such energetic activities, then alternatively, plan to get stuff done around the home. Make sure you are achieving so many tasks in a week to give yourself a sense of satisfaction, such as:

- Starting a hobby, ie card making, knitting, jigsaw puzzles.
- Gardening can be therapeutic and a great way to get yourself outside and fit.
- Bake, cakes, cupcakes biscuit and pies, whatever takes your fancy. Beware of the calories. Though you could always donate your baking to a charitable cause, a great way to lift your self-esteem.
- Having a luxurious soak in the bathtub with candles.
- If money is an issue for you, then take a serious look at your finances. By planning ahead, you may find yourself better off financially.
- Get up an hour earlier to get more done.

Whatever way you choose to approach your Activity Scheduling (AS), it is important that it gives you pleasure or satisfaction. AS is meant to serve as your own self-reward. If you plan to tackle that bill-paying session, the feel-good factor should come from knowing that you are tackling a problem. That, in itself, can ease anxiety. Plus, if you are addressing such problems, keep the time devoted to these tasks short. Problems are solved much better if broken up into smaller pieces.

Don't just include outside activities, add things that you keep putting off so you can have a sense of self-achievement. This type of therapy ties up well with creating a routine in your life. By planning some good things ahead, that you can do with your time, you will have less time to dwell on those negative anxious thoughts.

5. Mindfulness-based Cognitive Therapy (MBCT)

"A man is but the product of his thoughts. What he thinks, he becomes."—Mahatma Gandhi

Mindfulness is an activity often more related to Buddhist monks. Some may also relate it to the ancient practice of yoga. It is also a useful tool in CBT for treating stress-related disorders and anxiety. Whilst it is a meditative practice, it can help anyone to learn to focus on the inner self.

We are all capable of visually seeing what happens around us, but many of us cannot see what is happening within. By becoming more aware of your inner thoughts you can analyze how they fit into the world around you. It teaches you how to study your own emotions and question the reasons why you react to certain things. If you are more aware, then you can make better judgments. It is generally being aware of the 'self' in the "here and now that Mindfulness will help you to focus on.

Mindfulness has shown to be effective in helping to treat anxiety, stress, and depression. Goldin & Gross (2010) carried out a study on participants who suffered from Social Anxiety Disorder (SAD) (4.5a). The results indicated that their symptoms were reduced whilst participating in mindfulness exercises.

American professor, emeritus of medicine, Jon-Kabat Zin is the pioneer of Mindfulness-Based Stress Reduction (MBSR) (4.5b). He opened a Stress Reduction clinic in 1979. It runs 8-week courses on Mindfulness-based Cognitive Therapy, based on MBSR. MBSR uses a combination of mindfulness meditation, yoga, and personal body awareness. This helps to treat issues such as pain management, anxiety and also reduces stress. MBSR has proven to be so effective that mindfulness meditation is taught in almost 80% of all medical schools in the US.

People mostly react automatically to stimulus, often not giving much thought to their response. This is known as Automatic Negative Thoughts (ANTs).

For Example Road rage can develop from a very minor incident. Perhaps someone cuts you up on the highway and you automatically sound your horn. Why have you done this? It is not meant to be used aggressively. Yet, you are letting the driver know you are not happy with what they have done. This can further develop into a more aggressive situation. You then speed-up to catch them. Further, you then outstare them or even worse, you might force them to stop and physically confront them. The behavior serves no purpose. Instead, you will succeed in raising your own blood pressure and elevating your stress levels as your anger increases.

The exaggerated behavior developed from your unconsciousness. That is because it is a part of your automatic thought process. A reaction you have developed over the years for a disagreeable event. The incidence led to your thoughts becoming fuelled by your emotions. In turn, this led to your aggressive behavior.

MBCT sessions would help you to become more aware of your present senses, and avoid such scenes in the future. You will learn to recognize certain indicators. The fact that your heart speeds up and you grip at the wheel tightly, should alert you to the imminent danger. Because you have learned to look out for such signals, you will no longer respond automatically. Instead, you will purposely intervene and alter your reaction. it will give you the power to hold back on your previous aggressive behavior. Your alternative thinking will be more on the terms of: The guy cut out in front of me but he's done it now. No point exploding with anger and making myself ill when it won't change that fact. Your new automatic reaction will be to take some deep breaths and force your hands to relax on the wheel.

Relaxation Exercises in MBCT

By using basic meditation exercises, it empowers you to ease any imminent anxiety attacks.

Breathing 4-7-8

This is a relaxation method that you can use anywhere, anytime. Though it is also a form of yogic breathing as it leads to relaxation for a meditation session. It's always better if you can lay down, or sit, but you can do it standing up if that becomes necessary.

- Close your eyes if possible. It helps to shut out the visual noise that you can see.
- Inhale deeply through your nostrils for the count of 4.
- As you inhale, allow your abdomen to expand, you will find that your chest also rises.
- Hold the breath for the count of 7.
- Gently exhale the air through an open mouth for the count of 8.
- Repeat this process until you feel a calmness.
- Use different rates of counting if 4-7-8 doesn't work for you or makes you feel dizzy.

It can take a while to adjust the "count" to your own body but 4-7-8 is a general rule of thumb. The hardest part is focussing on cutting out the busy world around you. Once you achieve this skill you will be capable of switch off momentarily. Not only will the panic pass over but you should also experience an inner peace.

A study by Brown & Gerbarg (2005), show that at least 30 minutes of daily yogic exercise a day, helps to reduce the symptoms of stress, anxiety and PTSD (4.5c).

Progressive Muscle Relaxation

This is another exercise that will have better results if you can lay down. Though it can be done seated or standing up if you find yourself in a stressful situation, but there will be limitations.

The idea behind this technique is to relax muscles in your body. It is also known as a body scan as you can start from the bottom of the body to the top, or vice versa. It is always better if you begin any exercise by using the breathing method to begin with.

- Close your eyes if possible to shut out the visual noise that you can see.
- Inhale deeply through your nose, hold for a few seconds before exhaling through your mouth.
- Concentrate on your feet. Flex and wiggle them, tighten any muscles. Move the toes and turn the ankles.
- If you have the time, complete the breathing exercise before moving on to the next muscle group, though it isn't necessary if you don't.
- Next, think only about your lower legs and calves, tensing and then relaxing any muscles in that area.

- Use this method to work your way through your body until you arrive at your face.
- Tighten any muscles in the face area by screwing up your eyes and wiggling your nose. Open the jaws wide a few times and gently wiggle it from side to side. Feel your face muscles relaxing as you do so.
- Finish with a few deep breathing exercises before you open your eyes to the world around you.

If you do this in public you may find yourself only focusing on a few muscle groups. At least you are shifting your thoughts from the anxiety and focusing on the inner self. That is the whole intention, to try and eliminate those negative thoughts by using a deep meditative means of relaxation.

Such exercises will have a positive effect on your wellbeing.

6. Altering Negative Thought Patterns
Low Self Esteem

It is not unusual to find that a person suffering from anxiety, will also usually suffer from low self-esteem. The chances are they have put themselves down in their own minds. This is a natural way of thinking as their confidence has diminishes. Low self-self-esteem can be a direct result of maladaptive thoughts.

There are some steps that you can take to try and overcome negative thought patterns. Let's have a look at a few of these ideas:

A trigger point can occur simply by you perceiving a remark by someone else, to be negative. If you find yourself feeling upset at another's remark, learn to recognize why you are upset. Take action by not allowing the maladaptive thought to fester. Don't give it time to build up, as this can create a snowball effect of anxiety. One way to do that is to try and relax internally. Use the breathing techniques we discussed earlier. Even if it's only to close your eyes for a few seconds. Try and at least inhale one deep breath through your nose, and exhale the air through your mouth. It is enough to take your mind away from an instant automatic reaction.

Case Scenario:

Let's suppose you are in a meeting and feel excited at doing your own presentation. Your mood is good and positive. Then someone comes at you with what you perceive as an insulting remark. Whilst you take that deep breath, think about the situation you are in. To help you understand why the remark triggered a negative thought ask yourself: -

- Is it the person rather than the remark?
- Would you have felt the same no matter who had said that same remark?
- Have they actually made a valid point?
- Did you experience a mood swing as soon as the trigger point happened?

By using our example, we know that the person felt happy and confident only moments before the comment. When they received the negative remark, they felt annoyed and upset.

Automatic Thoughts

If an instant mood swing does happen, it means that you have experienced an "automatic thought. Most automatic thoughts are instant negative responses. Again, be aware and ask yourself: -

- Am I now thinking negative remarks detrimental to my self-confidence, such as "I'm useless at this," or "that person never liked me?"
- Look for evidence in your mind that might support why you had such an automatic negative response.

By asking yourself such questions, it forces you to look objectively at the automatic thought process. Is there any evidence to support why you are now thinking about this person in a negative way? Or, is their point a good one?

The remark caught you unawares and unprepared. Before you use an automatic response, assess the situation in your mind as fast as you can. By learning to see your own trigger points, such as this one, you will know when not to respond immediately. The last thing you want is to come across as aggressive, so stop and think. As you are busy analyzing the situation in your mind, it allows for a short pause. that's a good thing as you are not responding instantly. It brings to mind the saying, "Think before you speak."

Positive Thinking

Bring in some positive thinking too, for example:

- Only one person raised any comments, so that's not too bad.
- I can't be useless if I'm standing here doing a presentation of my ideas.

If you manage to stay calm and answer the question sensibly, then pat yourself on the back. You've managed to challenge those automatic and maladaptive thoughts. Now you can approach the objector calmly and not make a fool of yourself. Your response can be a measured one because you have taken full control of your thinking.

This is only a simple example. It reflects a situation that would need to be performed on the spot, to stop any automatic negativeness.

Beware when you are feeling vulnerable and want to snap at someone for something they said. Pause and ask yourself: -

- Am I having an instant thought and reaction?
- Has what they said caused a swing in my mood and emotions?
- Can I stay calm and smile and stop assuming negative stuff in my head?

If you have decided to do a journal and something like this happens in your day, take notes. What was the situation that forced your automatic negative reaction? What was your instant mood when it happened? How did you deal with it? When you get a chance, look at your notes to analyze them to see if you could have changed anything. Learn from the experience, don't ignore it. Learn to master the process of pausing to analyze. It is a start to your challenging all maladaptive thoughts, in all situations.

7. Anxiety in Childhood

We have discussed how adults can challenge negative thought patterns that lead to anxious thoughts. What then of children? Can a child suffer from anxiety?

The answer to that is, yes. Whilst it's quite difficult to gain exact scientific data from this age group, nonetheless, children do suffer from anxiety. One such study by Muris and Broeren (2009) (4.7a), looked at research taken over 25 years. The results indicated that in fact anxiety disorders, including PTSD, OCD, and social phobias, are on the increase for the young. Given this daunting news, how can we help our children to cope with a condition that few adults can manage to handle?

How do you know if your own child is suffering from anxious moments?

There are a few signs in a child's behavior that could indicate anxiety is present.

- Tiredness that is probably due to lack of sleep.
- Suffering panicky scared feelings for much of the time.
- Lack of concentration, leading to poor school performance.
- Misbehaving.
- Taking tantrums.
- Bullying other children.
- Withdrawal from play.
- Constant complaints of tummy aches or headaches.

Some of these symptoms can also be signs of general childhood ailments. Though if they are frequent and persistent, then anxiety may be the cause.

Anxiety is the most common mental health ailment for young people. Community studies show that between 9-32% of children and adolescents suffer some form of anxiety disorder. (Creswell, Waite & Cooper 2014) (4.7b). This can and does have an adverse effect on their development. The research sadly indicates that anxiety in childhood can continue into adulthood. Anxiety issues affect a child's family life, social development, and educational achievement. It can even result in dependence on welfare and low paid employment, later in adulthood. (Piacentini & Robleck 2002) (4.7c). Many children suffering from anxiety disorders go untreated because the symptoms are so variable.

Genes also play their part in anxiety. Studies are showing that if you have a close relative suffering a Generalized Anxiety Disorder (GAD), then you are seven times more likely to suffer it too. (Turner, Beildal & Costello 1987) (4.7d). Genetics do not offer a complete explanation. The social environment of a child plays a huge role. For example, if children witness their parents' anxious behavior, they are more likely to mirror such emotions. Difficult and upsetting experiences are another factor. That can include the death of a family member or a loved pet, or being subject to violence or abuse. These situations can lead to PTSD, which can have a devastating effect on anyone, let alone a child. There is a range of specific, seemingly innocuous moments in a child's life, that can result in the onset of anxiety. Such as Separation Anxiety when starting school. Most children do well in a good routine, so when their regular day altered, it can cause them anxieties.

How do we treat anxiety in children?

Treatment for children is not that different to the treatment for adults. The premise is the same; identify maladaptive thoughts and challenge them. Intervention as early as possible is more likely to see a better success rate from the treatment. Delayed treatment carries a risk of the child becoming isolated. If that happens they may become unable to cope and fall behind in their development.

Supportive parents, teachers, and friends play a major role in a child's life. Learning to recognize a child's trigger points is a great way forward in therapy. To do this, some children may be treated with Exposure therapy. It does not need to be a direct exposure, as in-vivo exposure. A more suitable method for children is imaginal exposure. It is useful in helping to alter maladaptive thinking, the same way as it does for adults.

Providing support to talk about and confront their fears is another method. It encourages them to discuss their fears with you, so together you can find solutions to reduce that fear.

Other treatment options include Modeling. This is where a

model, usually the therapist, acts out the behavior which is causing the anxiety in the child. The child learns by observations, though Modeling alone has a short-term effectiveness. When combined with role-play and positive reinforcement exercises, it is more successful. Role-play is a way of rehearsing with coping mechanisms. It will involve challenging the negative thoughts and at the same time rewarding the child for correct behavior. this has been taken forward with the use of computer-assisted CBT. A study by Khanna & Kendall (2010) (4.7e), showed that by using computer-aided CBT with children, it was very effective in reducing anxiety.

CBT has proven to be a useful treatment for children, even very young children. A study by Minde et. al. (2010) (4.7d), shows that children between the ages of 3-7 suffering anxiety disorders can still benefit with CBT.

In a clinical setting, they will build their skills in altering thought patterns. The patients will also be given tasks for homework, where their supporters can become involved too. Parents can also be directed into changing their approach to the child. They too may need to learn new tactics and coping strategies. Considering that parents are the role models, it is important to train them as well.

With the use of CBT, the patient can look forward to a quick recovery. By the end of a few months of therapy sessions, the child should learn new coping strategies for their future. The average therapy sessions required can be between 8-16. Some patients may need more, dependent on the severity of their symptoms. With the coping skills taught in CBT, and support from immediate family members, the outlook for these children is very good. That is not true though for a child who goes untreated. The likelihood is that they will continue to suffer anxiety and maladaptive thoughts. Untreated, their condition will most likely get worse as they get older.

Chapter 5 Exposure Therapy

Anxious Fears

Exposure therapy is a CBT technique used for helping people who suffer various anxiety disorders and phobias. Research of this technique has shown that when provided by a skilled practitioner it is both effective and safe.

Exposure therapy is used mainly to treat:
- Post-Traumatic Stress Disorder (PTSD)
- Panic attacks

- Obsessive-compulsive Disorder (OCD)
- Social Anxiety Disorder (SAD)
- Generalized Anxiety Disorder (GAD)

The history of exposure therapy predates CBT. It was initially a method of treatment prescribed by behavioral psychologists. The foundation of which was based on classical conditioning. The most famous classical conditioning experiment was Ivan Pavlov's experiment with dogs. He conditioned them to salivate at the sound of a bell, as that preceded the introduction of food.

Behavioral psychologists, such as B.F. Skinner, took this principle further. The introduction of operant conditioning was an additional concept of modifying certain behaviors. Skinner believed behavior was determined by consequences, whether good or bad. The consequences then determine if the behavior continues, or not. Positive consequences result in reinforcing the behavior. Whilst negative consequences would, for most people, result in the cessation of such behavior.

It was Mary Cover Jones, often described as the mother of behavior therapy, who introduced the concept of desensitization. This is a process of repeatedly exposing a person to the stimulus that is the cause their anxiety. Today we know this as exposure therapy.

Fear is a powerful emotion. When we fear something, it is only natural that we try and avoid it. For certain situations it is acceptable, such as you would not confront a big bear on purpose. In a more realistic setting, some people may be frightened of driving at excessive speeds so avoid that situation. Another reasonable and practical fear. It is when your fears focus on the more mundane situations that it is considered a problematic type of fear. Perhaps being in an enclosed space, or being in a crowd. Avoiding everyday situations can have a detrimental effect on your quality of life. Avoiding situations that make you unwell, may at first seem the right thing to do. It seems a sensible option to help ease your anxious feelings. What such avoidance is really doing though, is reinforcing the fear. If you don't tackle the problematic fear, you can never overcome it.

Exposure therapy is intent on breaking that cycle of avoidance so that it will not be so maladaptive. This type of therapy has variations of methods. They are tailored by the therapist to suit the individual's needs.

Common Exposure Methods

In-Vivo Exposure

A treatment path which directly exposes the suffer to the stimuli. This would be carried out under the supervision of a trained therapist and is about confronting the fear. An example could be a client who has an inhibiting fear of flying. One aspect of the treatment could involve them visiting an airport and actually boarding a plane. They will not do this alone as they will be accompanied by a trained therapist. Throughout the event the client is encouraged to practice calming techniques, such as controlled breathing.

Interoceptive Exposure

A technique whereby the therapist induces physical sensations. This is encouraging the client to think about and describe their fear. Such physical feelings may include shortness of breath, muscle tension, and a racing heartbeat. The purpose is to show that these sensations, while uncomfortable, are not actually dangerous.

Imaginal Exposure

Often used in a complementary fashion to In Vivo Exposure.

The difference being that it uses Imaginal Exposure. The client is not exposed directly to the situation that causes their anxiety. Instead, they are encouraged to visualize the traumatic fear. Similar to Interoceptive Exposure, the intent is to provoke the feelings of anxiety.

Virtual Reality Exposure

This is a new technique. It involves immersing the patient in a virtual reality environment, usually with a headset. It is ideal for exposing a client to certain situations that they perceive as dangerous in the real world. Particularly useful for those suffering PTSD and has been successful with combat veterans.

An important element to using exposure therapy is determining the level of exposure to the anxiety-inducing stimuli. Too much too soon may be damaging to the client. There are three basic methods of determining exposure levels in CBT.

Systematic Desensitization

Exposure to the anxiety-inducing stimuli, while engaging in stress-reducing activities. This would include exercises such as controlled breathing, or other relaxation techniques.

Graded Exposure

With the help of the therapist, the client is asked to construct a hierarchal list of anxiety-inducing situations. This treatment will involve exposing the client to the less threatening fears first. Then, a build-up to the more difficult situations at a gradual pace.

Flooding

This is a more aggressive and somewhat controversial method of exposure therapy. That is because this method overwhelms the client with anxiety-inducing stimuli. Whilst it can only be used on a limited number of clients, it is perhaps the most cost-effective and quickest method. It has proven to help cure phobias and other anxiety issues.

Does exposure therapy work?

There has been a plethora of studies showing this method of therapy is successful in helping people with anxiety issues. How successful it is for each individual person, is dependent on the therapist's approach. One such study by Rothbaum & Schwartz (2002) (5a), demonstrates that it is successful in treating PTSD. For most, a gradual approach is key to success. If it is not rushed into it and taken one step at a time, the patient can overcome the sense of dread that they feel.

Following are some examples of how different techniques in exposure therapy can help treat PTSD:

PTSD Sufferers have either been the victim of a traumatic event or witnessed one. Typical symptoms of PTSD can include repetitive disturbing thoughts and frightening nightmares. As they play the event over in their minds, it can make them hyper-vigilant, (always on the lookout for danger). All these symptoms can lead to depression.

Like most anxiety issues, those suffering from PTSD can take the same route for relief, which is often avoidance. This is counter-productive, as avoidance reinforces the fear, it can also lead to other problems. Those supplementary issues can include emotional detachment from others, even loved ones. Along with a lack of interest in life and again depression will set in. Exposure therapy for PTSD can take many forms. By using that various techniques we have mentioned earlier, see how they fit in to a PTSD patient's therapy:

In-Vivo Exposure

The patient is exposed to the event that causes the anxiety. This might involve visiting the scene of the traumatic event. For example, someone involved in a violent incident could visit the place where it happened. A professional therapist will guide them to challenge the feelings that arise. It must be a supervised situation as the patient can become overwhelmed, needing to leave the scene immediately.

Imaginal Exposure

If the patient is not yet ready to face the scene of the event, then this is a safer option. Instead, the patient uses imaginary techniques to relive the traumatic experience. It will be necessary to relive the experiences in their mind. Along with a professional therapist who will help them to challenge the thoughts and feelings that this memory can bring about.

Interoceptive Exposure

A typical symptom of PTSD can come in the form of a panic attacks. Such attacks are often in response to a physical sensation, such as a racing heart, or shortness of breath. With this technique, the therapist will try and induce those feelings. This is done by encouraging the patient to hyperventilate. It can be used in conjunction with Imaginal Exposure. The patient not only imagines the event but is also experiencing induced hyperventilation. A study by Wald & Taylor (2008) (5b), shows that Interoceptive Exposure is effective in reducing anxiety in PTSD sufferers.

Virtual Reality Exposure

This method is becoming increasingly popular. Most especially for treating armed forces veterans, as well as active soldiers. PTSD is a known condition that can be brought on by combat memories. It is about replicating anxiety-inducing scenarios, without placing the client in physical danger. This can involve immersing the client into a virtual reality world that is created with powerful computers. The patient experiences not only a visual world but also other senses too. It will include audio, and sometimes sensory awareness of touch. The visual and audio sensations are translated via a headset. Whilst the sensory sensations are experienced by sensors placed around the patient's body. Like all exposure therapy, the intention is to repeatedly expose the client to the anxiety-inducing stimuli. Eventually, the autonomic arousal that is a causal factor in panic attacks, is subdued. This is known as "habituation." Virtual Reality Exposure has shown to be successful in helping PTSD suffers. It works at reducing the severity of their PTSD symptoms.

Exposure therapy is a useful tool at helping to treat those who suffer PTSD. It can also help with other anxiety issues, such as phobias and Obsessive Compulsive Disorders. The various techniques offer ways to challenge the maladaptive thought process. In the long run, it helps patients to come to terms with the trauma that caused the illness in the first place. The origins of this type of therapy are based on older forms of behavioral psychology. But, as in Virtual Reality Exposure, it has been developed to help patients deal with modern day issues. All of which are possible with by the new state of the art technology.

Chapter 6 Formulating and executing a personalized plan

Self Help Treatment for Anxiety Disorders

If you are an anxious person and it affects your life in a debilitating way, then you do need to take action. The best way forward would be to seek a professional CBT therapist. If for some reason you cannot take that route, such as financial reasons or time, then there are alternatives. One option is self-help. This can be successful for none-extreme anxiety issues. Self-help healing has shown to be effective and can help to change your life around. (Hirai & Clum 2006, (6a). It is worth pursuing if only for your loved ones. Though, at the end of the day, you are the important one in this dilemma.

Remind yourself that you are not alone with your condition. The Anxiety and Depression Association of America (ADAA), informs us that around 15 million Americans suffer from Generalized Anxiety Disorder (GAD). On top of that, around 7.7 million Americans suffer PTSD. In the US 40% of adults will suffer from an anxiety disorder at some time in their lives (ADAA 2013) (6b).

By becoming your own therapist you are taking the first step to tackling your anxiety issues. Depression can be a more difficult condition to tackle because of its deep routed causes, but self-help can still be useful. A meta-analysis of 34 studies by Gellatly et. al. (2006) (6c), looked at the effectiveness of self-help for depression. They found that self-help could successfully reduce the symptoms.

CBT involves learning ways of challenging the negative thoughts the lead to anxiety. Further practice is then required for a well-balanced mental health outlook. By reading books like this one you may have already identified that you are experiencing a problem you want to deal with. After all, this is not a topic that makes good bedtime reading. However, by reading material on CBT therapy, you have made the right start.

CBT is such a logical way of tackling anxiety issues. That is because it forces the practitioner to face their anxieties and do something about them. Once you have admitted that you need to tackle some issues you are having, then it is time to move on:

- What are your negative inner thoughts?

- Whilst focusing on those thoughts, note the moods and emotions you feel whilst you are thinking them.
- Compare your moods to how you feel when you're not thinking those thoughts.
- Learn how to dissect such thoughts, as discussed in the various CBT methods throughout this book.

Research and Reading Material

There is a rich variety of reading materials around, both online and in physical book format. Read about the different CBT methods, such as the breathing techniques. Then have a go at putting them into practice.

Putting a CBT Method into Practice

Find a CBT technique that suits you, such as writing a journal which is ideal for busy people. Writing a contemporaneous daily record allows you to read it later on. This allows you to reflect on situations that made you anxious during your day. Did something happen at the office that upset you? If you had a chance to log down your thoughts at the time, later when you have calmed down you can analyze why it made you anxious and take action.

Time Management

The word "management" can bring to mind something you do in a working situation, but you can implement this into your personal life. Studies show that having an organized life can bring about a feeling of fulfillment.

Those who suffer anxious moments should avoid being disorganized and rushing about everywhere. Rushing can lead to stress, which in turn starts a whole set of negative thoughts and emotions.

You do not need to have a strict regime, just one whereby your day is a little automated and everything gets done. Here are a few tips that can make a difference and give you empowerment of your life.

Rise earlier than you need to so you can begin your day half asleep. There is nothing worse than diving out of bed and rushing out of the house. Take your time while still dressed in your night clothes. Allow your brain to wake up at a slow pace. Have breakfast early, while you're still waking up. Lead on to a fresh shower and getting ready for the day. Lay your clothes out the day before so you don't need to think in the morning. By the time you leave your home, you will be refreshed and ready to embark on your journey to work.

If you need to travel, plan ahead. Look up the route and give yourself plenty of time. Remember, it is about being as calm and relaxed as possible.

Try to get into the habit of doing a week's meal planning, and then shopping only once during the week. That way everything is worked out ahead and you don't need to rush around when you get home. Plus, you will probably eat healthier if you think about the meals, rather than rushing into a take-out on the way home.

Problem solving

We all need to solve problems at various times in our lives. Sometimes they are the simplest of problems, such as what to wear. Other times they may be more life-changing. None of us can avoid having to make decisions. Most of the time it comes naturally.

When you have other factors in your life, such as money worries, making decisions can become a dreaded and difficult task. Train yourself to tackle problems by breaking them down into smaller portions. For example, if you are worrying that you can't pay all the bills, then you will soon become overwhelmed by the situation. Whereas, if you take the time to prioritize the bills, then action one at a time, you will begin to feel that you are tackling the overall situation.

It's important to keep on top of your life so you feel in control. If, for instance, you are avoiding a particular route to work because it is stressful, then practice Exposure Therapy. Introduce yourself to the route when it's not so busy. Maybe you could take a friend with you for the first time, for moral support.

Learn how to match up the different CBT methods to your own personal anxieties. That way you can begin to take back control of your life. Remember, take your time and don't rush any of the stages.

The Importance of Meditational Exercises

We have talked about this a few times, such as the breathing techniques. If you can incorporate these exercises into your life on a permanent basis, you will soon become familiar with your inner self. That is the person you are ultimately trying to help, so it is worth taking the time to get to know yourself better.

Facing Fears

If you do have phobias then try and get loved ones on board to help you. Don't go around your life avoiding everything. Confront it by using one of the CBT coping strategies. May even take time out of work so you can focus only on tackling the phobia, for a whole week.

CBT Worksheets

There are lots of free worksheets for the varying CBT methods, that can be found online. Do your research and find a few that you feel will be helpful to your particular anxiety. Share them with your loved ones so you have someone to discuss them with.

Key Tasks:

- Recognizing you have a problem.
- Focusing on your inner thoughts and challenging them.

- Finding ways to relax, particularly if you suffer panic attacks.
- Feeling in control of your life.

Then, it is a case of practicing your newfound skills and becoming stronger with your inner self.

Chapter 7 How to move on and continue

Life is one huge challenge, there is no denying that. Formal education in industrialized countries begins at a young age. Along with that comes the pressures to do well in our education. Already we are a part of the social structure of life, there is very little alternative to this way of life. We can have different beliefs and values, but still, the pressure to do well is ever present. Some choose not to live the "norm," but for most of us, we do our best to achieve what is expected of us.

As an adult comes the pressure to do well in a career. Added to that can be the stresses of raising a family, owning a home, a car, and all the latest gadgets that technology provides. We must dress in a certain way, and please our peer groups. This type of social pressure all plays its part upon our personal stress load. Deadlines to meet, places to be, money to earn, bills to pay. It is little wonder that we desire electronic gadgets for entertainment, just to help us unwind.

Whilst social structure is important to us, it does us no harm to step out of the rushing torrent of social expectations, every now and then. We take ourselves on vacation, but even that has to be paid for, organized and traveled to. Being on vacation can be stressful for some. This is where we need to think outside the box.

Most adults arrive at a breaking point sometime in their lives. With the pressures of life comes a price, and that is called stress. It can rear its ugly head in many forms, such as insomnia or eating disorders. The combination of these effects on our bodies floods us with the chemicals meant to protect us from danger. This can be the start of a downward spiral to depression. Of course there are many different reasons for worry and depression, but they all lead to the same result, making us ill.

That's why it's so important to know your own body, including your inner mind; to know yourself. Only then can you recognize the signs that you need help. CBT is a way of providing self-help, which is a great start on the road to recovery. Calming your emotions with meditational exercises is only the first step to healing. Turning around your negative thoughts is a little harder, and takes some time to become successful.

When you've come through a healing session of around 8-weeks, the goal then is to stay healed. There is no point in curing your anxieties only for them to resurface a few months down the line. It is so important to make sure you always recognize when stress is knocking on your door. Nip it in the bud before the symptoms escalate.

Maintaining a Healthy Outlook

If you've read through the chapters of this book, you will have an idea of how anxiety works on the body. How it can snowball into something that can become quite debilitating. When your body perceives a threat, messages go to the brain to produce a response which results in hormonal release. That's fine when faced with danger, it helps to keep you safe as you respond fast. When the body detects danger that is not real, those hormones become toxic.

Take back control by recognizing the signs of a panic attack that is not real. Use the meditational exercises to calm your body's emergency responses. It may sound unreal, but taking charge of your thoughts helps a great deal.

Once you are calmer, the emergency response of hormones will begin to shut down. It may take a few moments as you force your body to change direction, but it can be done. Relax those muscles. Convince your inner thoughts that there is nothing to panic about. Tell yourself that the world is still turning and everything around you remains normal.

Do this over and over until those attacks come less and less. Don't allow maladaptive thoughts to fuel your emotions. When you feel your body going into panic mode, stop whatever you are doing and take action, such as:-

- Close your eyes and start your breathing exercises.
- Visualize pleasant thoughts to distract your mind away from the panic.
- Count numbers in your head and keep counting to distract your mind into the mundane and away from the panic.
- If possible, sit or lay down and then relax go through the motions of tensing and relaxing muscles in your body.
- Go make a cup of tea or coffee to keep your mind distracted.
- Read a book as another form of distracting your thoughts away from the panic.

It is difficult to avoid stress and anxiety completely, but what you can do is recognize it and take action.

Other factors in your life can play a part in making sure that you feel happy inside:

- Spend as much time as you can with loved ones and friends.
- Smile more, even at yourself in the mirror.
- Take more short breaks if your day is a busy one.
- Take a look at your diet and cut down on those sugars and starches as much as you can.
- Take regular exercise, even if it's only walking.
- Visit somewhere pleasant.
- Sit on a bench and watch the world pass you by.
- Go somewhere and interact with nature to recharge your batteries.
- Take a good look at the world around you. Notice the little things like a bird in the sky, or an insect on the ground.
- Learn to appreciate the trees and flowers. Sometimes we rush everywhere in our cars and don't have time to notice that nature is all around us.

- Find time to talk to other people. After all, we are all going through the same processes. Learn to share your thoughts and others will share theirs with you. Be more tolerant of each other.
- Do kind things for other people around you. It does not need to involve money. You could smile at a complete stranger. You never know they may need it. Allow someone through a door before you step through it. Give up your seat on a train. Just add your helping hand around, if only for a few moments.
- Concentrate on "today." Not tomorrow or next week, only the here and now.
- Expect setbacks then they won't knock you down unexpectedly. They will happen; pick yourself up, brush yourself down and move on.
- Talk to yourself when no one's around. You are your best listener.

Perhaps you already practice some of our suggestions above. Learning to cope with anxious moments means re-training how you think. Once conquered, it is a new lifestyle that should stay with you for good. Think more positive thoughts and your smile will come naturally. That's because you have put stress and anxiety at bay.

Conclusion

At the beginning of this book, I set out to show you how CBT can be a successful treatment for curing anxiety. Mental health issues imbalance your thoughts. It is my hope that by trying some of these methods, you can learn to reach deep within yourself. By doing this you will begin to make major changes to your life. Mental health imbalances are debilitating to everyday life. The important factor here is that they are curable.

When we think of an illness, often we assume the treatment to be pharmaceutical or surgery. Rarely do we stop and understand that the cure could be the power of our own mind. This is where some may accuse us of entering the realms of spiritual practice. Yet, scientific studies show that we can physically alter the processes in our body, by using our minds.

When threatened with danger, it is only natural that the brain alerts the rest of our body to take the necessary action. But, sometimes we perceive a danger that isn't actually there. When that happens, the body begins the process of protection. By learning to recognize the autonomous reactions in your own body, you can learn how to control them. That is how easy it can be. Taking control of those maladaptive thoughts will completely alter your hormonal output. This is not rocket science, but it is medical facts on how the human body works.

CBT is not only successful in treating psychological conditions but medical ones too. It is proven to help with pain. A study by Yu, Norton & McCracken (2017) using a new technique in CBT called Acceptance and Commitment Therapy (ACT) helps with pain management (conc.a). Further CBT can also be effective in helping those who suffer from Insomnia. (Wagley et.al. 2012) . (conc.b).

You will not notice changes overnight. It takes practice to force your thoughts to go in a different direction. It takes practice to get those meditational exercises to kick in as soon as your body hits the alert button. These methods are life-changing. Once established, they can become a permanent part of living an anxiety-free existence.

References

6b) Anxiety and Depression Association of America, (2013) Available at https://adaa.org/about-adaa/press-room/facts-statistics, accessed 10-12-2018.

1b) Chiang KJ, Tsai JC, Liu D, Lin CH, Chiu HL, Chou KR. Efficacy of cognitive-behavioral therapy in patients with bipolar disorder: A meta-analysis of randomized controlled trials {published online May 4, 2017]. PLoS One.doi:10.1371/journal.pone.0176849

1c) Beutel ME, Stark R, Pan H, et al. Changes of brain activation pre- post short-term psychodynamic inpatient psychotherapy: an fMRI study of panic disorder patients. Psychiatry Res. 2010;184:96-104

4.2b) Boelen, P. A., de Keijser, J., van den Hout, M. A., & van den Bout, J. (2007). 'Treatment of complicated grief: A comparison between cognitive-behavioral therapy and supportive counseling.' Journal of Consulting and Clinical Psychology, 75(2), pp 277-284.

4.4a) Brian C. Chu; Daniela Colognori; Adam S. Weissman; Katie Bannon (2009) 'An Initial Description and Pilot of Group Behavioral Activation Therapy for Anxious and Depressed Youth', Cognitive and Behavioral Practice, ISSN: 1077-7229, Vol: 16, Issue: 4, Page: 408-419

4.5c). Richard P. Brown and Patricia L. Gerbarg Sudarshan Kriya Yogic Breathing in the Treatment of Stress, Anxiety, and Depression: Part II—Clinical Applications and Guidelines The Journal of Alternative and Complementary Medicine 2005 11:4, 711-717

4.2a) Bryant, R. A., Moulds, M. L., Guthrie, R. M., Dang, S. T., & Nixon, R. D. V. (2003). 'Imaginal exposure alone and imaginal exposure with cognitive restructuring in treatment of posttraumatic stress disorder.' Journal of Consulting and Clinical Psychology, 71(4), 706-712.4.2b)

4.7b) Creswell C, Waite P, Cooper PJ (2014) Assessment and management of anxiety disorders in children and adolescentsArchives of Disease in Childhood 2014;99:674-678

6c) Gellatly, J., Bower, P., Hennessy, S., Richards, D., Gilbody, S., & Lovell, K. (2007). What makes self-help interventions effective in the management of depressive symptoms? Meta-analysis and meta-regression. Psychological Medicine, 37(9), 1217-1228. doi:10.1017/S0033291707000062

4.5a Goldin P. R., Gross J. J. (2010). Effects of mindfulness-based stress reduction (4.5a). (MBSR) on emotion regulation in social anxiety disorder. Emotion 10, 83–91. 10.1037/a0018441

1a) Grossman P, Niemann L, Schmidt S, Walach H. Mindfulness-based stress reduction and health benefits. A meta-analysis. J Psychosom Res. 2004;57(1):35-43

2c) Hackett RA, Kivimäki M, Kumari M, Steptoe A. Diurnal cortisol patterns, future diabetes, and impaired glucose metabolism in the Whitehall II Cohort Study. J Clin Endocrinol Metab. 2016;101(2):619-625.

6a) Harai, M. & Clum GA. (2006), 'A meta-analytic study of self-help interventions for anxiety problems' Behav Ther. 2006 Jun;37(2):99-111

4.7e) Khanna, SM, and Kendal PC (2010) Computer-Assisted Cognitive Behavioral Therapy for Child Anxiety: Results of a Randomized Clinical Trial, Journal of Consulting and Clinical Psychology, 2010, Vol. 78, No. 5, 737–745

4.1a) Kirkham, A. J. Breeze J.M. Paloma, M.B. (2011) 'The impact of verbal instructions on goal-directed behaviour' Acta Psychologica Volume 139, Issue 1, January 2012, pp 212-219

4.7d) Minde K, Roy J, Bezonsky R, Hashemi A. The effectiveness of CBT in 3–7 year old anxious children: Preliminary data. J Can Acad Child Adolesc Psychiatry. 2010;19:109–15.

2a) McAuley MT, Kenny RA, Kirkwood TB, Wilkinson DJ, Jones JJ, Miller VM (March 2009). "A mathematical model of aging-related and cortisol induced hippocampal dysfunction". BMC Neuroscience. 10: 26. doi:10.1186/1471-2202-10-26. PMC 2680862. PMID 19320982.

4.7a) Muris, P. & Broeren, S (2008) 'Twenty-five Years of Research on Childhood Anxiety Disorders: Publication Trends Between 1982 and 2006 and a Selective Review of the Literature' J Child Fam Stud. 2009 Aug; 18(4): 388–395.

conc.a). Yu, L. Norton, S. & McCracken L.M. Change in "Self-as-Context" ("Perspective-Taking") Occurs in Acceptance and Commitment Therapy for People With Chronic Pain and Is Associated With Improved Functioning The Journal of Pain, Volume 18, Issue 6, 664 - 672

4.7c) Piacentini J, Roblek T. Recognizing and treating childhood anxiety disorders. West J Med. 2002;176:149–151. doi: 10.1136/ewjm.176.3.149.

2b) de Quervain DJ, Roozendaal B, McGaugh JL (August 1998). "Stress and glucocorticoids impair retrieval of long-term spatial memory". Nature. 394 (6695): 787–90. Bibcode:1998 Natur.394.787D. doi:10.1038/29542. PMID 9723618

5a) Barbara Olasov Rothbaum and Ann C. Schwartz Exposure Therapy for Posttraumatic Stress Disorder American Journal of Psychotherapy 2002 56:1, 59-75

4.5b). Tang, Yi-Yuan & Holzel, Britta & Posner, Michael. (2015). The neuroscience of mindfulness meditation. Nature Reviews Neuroscience. 16. 10.1038/nrn3916.

4.7d) Turner SM, Beidel DC, Costello A. Psychopathology in the offspring of anxiety disorder patients. Journal of Consulting and Clinical Psychology. 1987;55:229–235.

conc.b). Wagley, J. N., Rybarczyk, B., Nay, W. T., Danish, S. and Lund, H. G. (2013), Effectiveness of Abbreviated CBT for Insomnia in Psychiatric Outpatients: Sleep and Depression Outcomes. J. Clin. Psychol., 69: 1043-1055.

5b) Jaye Wald & Steven Taylor (2005) 'Interoceptive Exposure Therapy Combined with Trauma-related Exposure Therapy for Post-traumatic Stress Disorder: a Case Report,' Cognitive Behaviour Therapy 34:1, 34-40

Dialectical Behavior Therapy For Anxiety

Why Worry, Panic, PTSD And Other Anxiety Symptoms Can Finally Be A Problem Of Your Past

By

Jonathan Moran

Introduction

A woman entered into the doctor's office looking a bit haggard. She was a well-dressed lady with well-formed features, but the tenseness around her mouth and eyes kept her from seeming attractive. She glanced at the doctor nervously, not meeting his gaze as she entered in. She sat at the edge of the chair in an extremely awkward position, shifting her position every minute.

"So, Marie," the doctor said when they had finished their introductions. *"How may I help you?"*

She paused for a moment. *"I.. I think I am losing my senses."*

"Really? Why do you think so?" The doctor inquired.

"I keep getting these anxiety attacks. I've actually had them for so many years. Something is wrong with me. I feel like I am slowly going crazy."

She continued to describe her attacks: abrupt spells of terror in shopping malls or tall buildings. A sudden, suffocating sense of panic that left her breathless. The attacks would strike without any warning and would force her to shut herself inside the house for days, and sometimes, even weeks.

As the session continued, Marie opened up about her life. Her relationship had just fallen apart when her spouse decided he couldn't live with her anymore leaving her with problems like anxiety and post-traumatic stress syndrome.

But this was not it.

Marie was afraid of flying. She used to avoid elevators and had trouble making phone calls at work. She was painfully uncomfortable in social gatherings and abhorred crowded places.

Just like Marie, there are thousands of people who suffer from chronic anxiety, stress, phobias, and post-traumatic stress syndrome. For such individuals, exquisite vulnerability to intense emotional pain disturbs their quality of life. The unrelenting misery makes thoughts like self-harm and suicide as some common forms of relief.

"Repeated treatment failure make the therapy itself evoke the feelings of hopelessness."

The treatment decisions in such circumstances are extremely complicated. Focusing on therapies that essentially attempt to change you may evoke panic since such efforts had failed previously. It may trigger feelings of shame or anger, especially at the implication that a change is likely.

On the contrary, if you attempt to accept the vulnerability and limitations, you would end up getting panicked as well. The non-stop efforts to strike the perfect balance- accepting your vulnerability while forcing a change- may wear you down.

"I cannot take this anymore. No matter what I do, nothing seems to change."

As you struggle with this inner chaos killing you bit by bit every minute, there is something that might just work. Dialectical behavior therapy (DBT) has evolved to help people struggling with depression, anxiety, and other sorts of emotional disturbances.

When you have complicated, severe problems and a history of multiple treatment failures, when the gut-wrenching misery makes suicide or self-harm seem like your only option, DBT can help manage the chaos.

What Makes This Book Different?

With an accessible writing style with a surefooted clinical explanation of how DBT can be used, *Dialectical Behavior Therapy* will help you learn how to go against the grain. It explains all essential insights in a stepwise manner, encompassing detailed information about anxiety, stress, worry, Traumatic stress syndrome, panic attacks, and social anxiety. It further discusses the relevance of mindfulness backed up by explicit guidance about how to develop it. Chapter by chapter, you will be able to appreciate how DBT and the specific interventions embedded within it can help you fight your demons and live a peaceful life.

Anxiety: Understanding the Specifics

Imagine yourself running down the road. You are afraid, something is following you. You can feel it overbearing you, it is chasing you, and you are aware that if it gets hold of you, it will destroy you. It doesn't matter where you run, it always follows; down every alley, across every road and it is still there just at your tail. You manage to sneak into a house and hide- but it still finds you. As you finally get a chance to glance back at it, you see that it is, in fact, a ferocious grizzly bear grumbling savagely, waiting to grasp you and tear you into pieces.

Exhaustion begins to overcome you. You have not been able to get rid of the bear despite running for so long. What can you possibly do? How can you escape a ferocious animal who is determined to prey on you? You take a right turn and finally see it: your salvation. Only ten yards ahead of you is a flagpole.

You will definitely be safe up there, out of the bear's reach. Without wasting another minute, you take a chance. You run with all the energy left in your feeble body. And you make it.

Climbing all the way to the top, you look back to see the bear below you.

A feeling of relief overtakes you as you realize that you have finally found a safe haven.

Suddenly, a feeling of panic overtakes you. You are at the top of a flagpole, so much high from the ground that it starts panicking you. One wrong move and you will be right in front of the very bear you have been trying to dodge for so long. You have to remain alert all the time to prevent this.

The above –mentioned scenario defines a dream, a dream symbolizing anxiety and anxiety-related disorders. It tells you how anxiety affects your mind- constantly alert, else you fail, always anxious to a certain degree. Unfortunately, a lot of people are living this life today.

What is it?

Anxiety is a feeling of nervousness, unease, or worry about something for which there is no certain outcome. Millions of individuals across the world suffer from it. 20 million people in the United States are estimate to suffer from an anxiety disorder. [1]

To know what anxiety actually is, let's make up a little scenario.

Close your eyes and imagine yourself on a beach on a bright, sunny afternoon. The rays of the sun are penetrating your body in a pleasant way and you can feel the cool breeze swiftly touching your body. The sounds of nature are filling your air as you laugh with your family and friends. There are people around you who love you and you love them. You feel contented, happy, cozy, and anxiety-free.

Now imagine a completely different picture. It is past midnight and you are walking down a dark alley all by yourself. With doorways on either side, it crosses your mind how anyone could be hiding in there ready to pounce at you any time. Your hearing and vision become more sensitive and you find yourself pinpointing the slightest sound or movement. Your heart starts pounding, your breathing rate increases, and you start feeling dizzy and lightheaded. You badly need to throw up. You feel like your whole body is getting charged up with energy. It is full of anxiety and ready to face the music.

These two scenes depict the two ends of the anxiety scale. In the first scenario, you feel safe, secure, and warm. In the second, you are tensed up, highly alert, and afraid.

Anxiety serves many purposes in your body, the two most important ones being the following:

1. It helps your body prepare for a fight or flight response. You can go from being fully relaxed to all tense within a moment. Your body re-directs the resources to the major group of muscles (such as those in your chest, arms, and legs) in order to provide them with energy and prepare you for action. This is what causes the physical symptoms of anxiety- such as fast breathing, racing heartbeat, shakiness, and jitteriness- to appear.

2. Anxiety helps you plan ahead for any imminent dangers and enables you to deal with them. It is an excellent survival strategy but with an unfortunate side effect i.e. it makes you anxious and nervous just thinking about any situation.

What this means is that anxiety is actually a subconscious way through which humans evolved to protect themselves. It is normal for people to exhibit anxiety-related patterns sometimes. Behaviors like disturbing thoughts, frustration, checking, and a need for perfection are more common than you think.

Just think about it. How many supposedly "normal" people:

- Get a drink before going to a social function?
- Constantly check doors, switches, and windows?
- Try not to get involved in activities that involve public speaking?

You look at someone and wonder how they have so much more confidence than you ever do, but this can be delusional. In fact, confidence exists on numerous levels. Some people are extremely confident in some situations but in many other circumstances, they are not. It all depends on how you well you control your anxiety.

"Those with a high level of confidence may have as many or more weaknesses than those with low self-esteem. The difference is
this; instead of dwelling on their handicaps, they compensate for
them by dwelling on their strengths" (Alan Loy McGinnis)

Symptoms of Anxiety

Now that you have grasped the concept of anxiety, it is time to learn about its symptoms. Most of the symptoms related to anxiety are linked with dealing with and/or avoiding danger at three levels: your mind, behavior, and body. [2]

The Body

- Increased breathing rate
- Tachycardia (increased heart rate)
- 'butterflies' in the stomach
- Increased urinary urgency
- Lightheadedness and dizziness
- Feeling unwell or sick most of the time
- Xerostomia (dryness of the mouth)
- Problems in swallowing food
- Increased perspiration
- Increased jitters

The Mind

- The feeling of being scared
- A constant state of worry that you will embarrass yourself at a public place

- Constantly reminding yourself that you are unwell and sick, and may even die
- A constant feeling that everyone around you is observing every move you make
- A need to escape from your life in order to find a safe haven

The Behavior

- Making excuses just to avoid doing certain tasks
- Avoiding people/places that trigger anxiety
- Avoiding making social contact with others
- Relying on alcohol and other related agents before doing something that stresses you

Difference between Anxiety and Anxiety Disorders

We all feel anxious at times. Deadlines, relationships, being just on time for an appointment- you name it. There is plenty in life to worry about and it's completely normal to feel anxious at times. This actually helps you get out of the harm's way and prepare yourself for important situations.

But when people start experiencing persistent, excessive, irrational, and unrealistic anxiety that comes out every day for no reason at all and sticks around throughout the entire length of the day, they are suffering from generalized anxiety disorder.

As compared to anxiety, people suffering from anxiety disorders often expect the worst, even where this is no reason for it. This unrelenting worrying starts interfering with their everyday living. Physical symptoms often accompany which includes irritability, restlessness, fatigue, muscle tension, and difficulty in concentrating.

To understand the difference between anxiety and anxiety disorder more clearly, refer to the following table.

Anxiety	Anxiety Disorder
Worry about a stressful event like an upcoming exam or an assignment deadline/	A constant, unsubstantiated worry leading to stress, decreasing the interest in social activities and disrupting work/academic life.
Inability to relax or maintain focus while encountering a serious problem such as losing a job, feeling sick, or losing a loved one.	Constant feelings of Irritability, tenseness, and insomnia without any underlying reason.
Developing muscle aches, body fatigue, and tension due to certain situations like a bad day at college.	Restlessness, fatigue, and muscle aches persisting for 6 months straight with no logical reason at all.

The Link between Anxiety and Avoidance

Procrastination, excessive worry, and anticipation of the worst-case scenarios are a part of anxiety. These are the events of your mind. However, some people have the tendency to get adversely affected by anxiety, leading to increased physical sensations such as frequent outbursts of anger and panic attacks. They get stuck in a never-ending cycle of anxiety and the associated social avoidance. They get trapped in their own feelings and thoughts or frozen in fear just to get away from the apparent threat.

What do you do to escape such a situation? Avoid it all like plaque, or man up and face your fears?

You are probably aware of the phrase:

"Face your fear and do it anyway."

The idea behind it is simple. Confronting your fears allows you to tolerate adverse circumstances and helps you adapt and overcome your anxiety. However, in practice, most of the people prefer choosing avoidance. They start avoiding people, situations, and circumstances that induce anxiety, just to avoid suffering from their anticipated fears. Procrastination at work, keeping yourself distracted by other tasks, and excessive cleaning are also other forms of avoidance.

You can eventually learn to reverse these avoidance patterns by promoting self-awareness, recognizing the relevant triggers, and forcing yourself to face anxious situations of low levels so that you know how to handle them and adapt yourself according to them.

However, this only occurs in ideal situations. Most of the time, you end up getting stuck in a cycling series of fear. This never-ending cycle makes you fear your own feelings even more than the object of fear.

'The only thing you have to fear is fear itself.'

For instance, you are assigned to do a task your boss or a loved one, but you are scared that you may disappoint them because of your self-perceived incompetence. Because you are so scared of disappointing them, you may end up vandalizing the task in real. You might try burying the task or forgetting it; you may miss a deadline, or adopt a reckless attitude while finishing it. These are certain avoidance behaviors that are not essentially based on conscious choice. Rather, they occur in response to an underlying fright of being humiliated, judged, or called as a fraud.

In some situations, anxiety can also make you fear conflict forcing you to prevent an engagement in any problematic conversations or negotiating boundaries. During your childhood, you might have been taught to back-down or withdraw from a situation after a stressful event. However, remember that choosing to avoid situations will only make it hard for you to stand up for yourself. In other cases, choosing to avoid stressful situations may transform you into a people-pleasing person who always tries to keep them on the right side so that they do not confront you.

Attempting to dodge your fears by running away from tough situations may give you instant satisfaction and a sense of fulfillment. However, this will eventually make you compromise yourself and resent the people that you tried your best to please all your life.

As the patterns of avoidance repeat themselves, they become automatic and enforce anxiety and promote a feeling of helplessness. As people keeps avoiding every stressful situation that they encounters, he begins to lower their tolerance for adversity and risk associated with new circumstances. The more they run away, the more they develop negative associations. In addition to this, their brain latches onto certain unconscious sensory triggers that become inked with these situations. These triggers most commonly include crowded paces, claustrophobia, and making eye contact.

Anxious-avoidant behaviors can be considered as a series of negative reinforcement due to negatively rewarding behaviors. Instead of finding different means to adapt, anxiety forces you to hold back from any responsibility. This causes the establishment of a series of avoidance which keeps repeating itself in the form of a cycle. Hence, a negative reinforcement of all the situations that you fear develops. You sabotage your goals just to get instant gratification and avoid experiencing fear.

With every anxious situation you avoid, you are increasing the likelihood of avoiding them in the future. In this way, you keep cycling between anxiety and the consequent patterns of avoidance- *ad infinitum*.

Anxiety-related Problems

There are several conditions that commonly accompany anxiety. These conditions usually develop from the reasons you find- to explain your anxiety- and the ways you adopt to deal with it. These conditions can be expressed at three levels: physical, psychological, and behavioral.

Physical Conditions

- Headaches
- Fatigue
- Bowel problems
- Constant colds
- Allergic reactions
- Digestive problems
- Skin problems

Most of the conditions mentioned above are due to the malfunctioning of the body's immune cells due to certain chemicals released in the bloodstream due to anxiety.

Behavioral Conditions

- Social phobia: Doing things in front of others will make you panic-stricken.
- Generalized anxiety disorder: persistent, uncontrollable worry about people/situations/events.
- Avoidance Behavior: Avoiding any situation that scares you.
- Obsession Compulsion Disorder (OCD): characterized by uncontrollable thoughts and compulsions to control these thoughts by attempting to avoid any danger or threat.
- Depression: This involves a feeling of hopelessness and helplessness and a belief that you have lost the control over your life and cannot succeed at anything no matter how hard you try.
- Sexual Problems: The fear of being judged on your performance and thoughts of losing control can lead to sexual problems.
- Miscellaneous: It includes aggression, eating disorders, and sleep disorders.

Psychological Conditions

- Perfectionism: This involves a need to always be the strongest, the cleverest, or the most beautiful. It urges

you to do everything perfectly and be on the top of everyone else.
- Making Comparisons: Always comparing yourself to other people and coming up short.
- Self-consciousness: Constantly worrying about yourself/watching yourself.
- Child-like Behavior: Desperate to seek the approval and love of parents and other people
- Excessive Tidiness: This indicates attempts to keep everything in order and to gain a feeling of control over everything.
- Ending Sentences with Questions: This is an attempt to avoid others from focusing on you and divert their attention towards the other person.
- Fantasizing: Some of the most common fantasies include being famous, rich, or great someday.
- Symmetry: An obsession to maintain the symmetry in everything you do. For example, making sure that whatever happens to your body must be equally done on either side. The condition is also linked with the feeling of order and control.

Summary

Anxiety, its symptoms, the severity of these symptoms, the circumstances in which they hit you, and how they are related to one another each other can be complex. These symptoms may support each other and until they become a part of your make up. It is not surprising at all that you tend to use phrases like *"It is a part of me"* or *"this is who I am."*

But remember that at some point, even a sad person may gain happiness. A weak person at some point can be strong at some other point. It is possible for a scared and unconfident person to gain courage and confidence. In order to do this, you must nurture the positive vibes and get the bad ones in control. You do not need to be worried how little positivity you have in you, what really matters is that it exists!

"It takes but one positive thought when given a chance to survive and thrive to overpower an entire army of negative thoughts" (Robert H. Schuller)

Is it really possible to get rid of all the problems you are facing? Yes. The next section will help you develop an understanding about what it takes.

Dialectical Behavior Therapy: An Overview

Brenda, a woman in her early thirties, has severe anxiety that has not gotten better through all her past therapies. She would get panic attacks while riding the trains that sometimes prevented her from attending her sessions. She would isolate herself every other day, not reaching out to family or friends because she was afraid they might judge her and may not want to hear about her problems.

Brenda also has rocky relationships in general. She would break up with her boyfriend one day, then message him non-stop the very next day, begging him to get back with her.

A medical record of multiple treatment failures combined with the ineffectiveness of the current therapy, Brenda's therapist refers her for a more intensive treatment, a type of psychotherapy that often works when all other therapies have failed: Dialectical Behavior Therapy.

DBT has offered great success to a lot of clients. What is this therapy and why does it manage to succeed other methods don't?

What is DBT and How does it Work?

During the late 1970s, Dr. Marsha Linhan was attempting to use the standard Cognitive Behavioral Therapy (CBT) to help adult women suffering from suicidal ideation, repeated suicidal attempts, and an increased urge to self-mutilate or self-harm. Trained as a behaviorist, she was more interested in managing discrete behaviors; however, after consulting with colleagues, she finally came to realize that the women she intended to target met the criteria for Borderline Personality Disorder (BPD).

During the '70s, Cognitive Behavioral Therapy (CBT) received prominence as a beneficial psychotherapy and was used as the mainstay of all the treatment targeting behavioral problems. Linehan was eager to know if this therapy holds high functionality, specifically for people who had developed suicidal tendencies as a coping mechanism against shear stress and extreme pain.

As she along with her research team worked within the boundaries of CBT to help such individuals, lots of problems kept surfacing time after time. They found that CBT was associated with a high withdrawal and dropout rate in the middle of the sessions because of its unrelenting focus on change. The magnitude and severity of the problems that the clients presented with were unexpectedly high; sometimes so much that CBT failed to provide enough time for the therapists to go through the problems faced by their clients and conduct therapy sessions in order to sort them out.

To tackle these issues, the researchers decided to make some modifications to the standard principles of CBT. They came up with new strategies such as acceptance-based interventions and reformulated the basic structure of the treatment. The purpose of these interventions was to give confidence to the patients struggling with social unacceptability and to make them realize that whatever behavior they exhibited, even the ones involving self-mutilation and self-harm, had a well-formed reason. This also helped the therapists learn different ways to teach their clients when to trust their judgments and how to know that whatever they are doing makes sense. In this due course of acceptance, Linehan found another set of strategies- Dialectics- that could essentially help these clients even more.

As a DBT therapist, Lineham focused to adopt a dialectical worldview, with a strong focus on opposing perspectives.

This helped her blend the concept of change in the clients while making them accept their flaws acceptance in a balanced way. This ultimately led to a significant improvement in therapeutic movement, flow, and speed. Beyond the dialectical view, specific strategies used during the sessions prevented the clients from getting stuck in rigid feelings, judgments, thoughts, and behaviors that may occur when emotions are running high.

So, in an attempt to help women with BPD, Dr. Lineham finally landed on a DBT, a strategy which is currently helping people lots of people suffering from behavioral disorders. Dialectical behavior therapy (DBT), which refers to a type of talk therapy, encompasses a cognitive behavioral approach which includes an amalgam of the social factors in harmony with the individual behavior. What makes it different from CBT or any other conventional therapy is that it primarily uses the psychosocial concepts and aspects to help clients transition to a better place in life.

The main concept behind DBT is that for some people, the likelihood of reacting intensely towards a certain situation is higher than the others. DBT theory encircles around the fact that the arousal levels of some people under any triggering circumstances may heighten at a much faster pace than a normal person. Due to this reason, it is normal for such people to develop a higher degree of emotional stimulation and require a lot of time before they retouch the baseline levels.[3]

DBT operates on multiple levels simultaneously to help the patient get over their problems. But how does it accomplish this? The following three features highlight the mechanism through which DBT helps people:

It is Support Oriented

DBT helps the patients identify their strengths and build on them so that they feel better about themselves and their lives.

It is Cognitive-based

DBT helps the patients identify the beliefs, assumptions, and thoughts that are making their life harder. **"I am a terrible person if I get angry"** and **"I need to be perfect at everything I do**" are some of the thoughts that may haunt you making it extremely difficult to live life in a normal way.

DBT helps people learn different patterns of thinking and make their lives more bearable. In simpler words, it will help you be at peace with yourself and settle on thoughts like **"there is no need to be perfect at everything"** and **"anger is a normal emotion, everyone experiences it."**

It is Collaborative

DBT works on a continuous relationship between clients and staff. In this therapy, the patients are encouraged to sort out their life problems in collaboration with their therapists. It demands the people to role-play new methods of interacting with others, finish homework assignments, and rehearse skills like calming yourself when upset.

These skills form a crucial part of DBT and are taught to the patients in weekly lectures and homework groups. In this way, individual therapists help their clients master the skills of DBT and apply them to their lives.

Four Stages of DBT

The treatment with DBT is commonly broken down into four levels. The clients are assigned to any of these levels on the basis of the intensity of their behaviors. The therapists are instructed to follow the frame defined in these levels to help the clients. No specific timeframe has been allotted to these stages. The therapist and clients are allowed to spend as much time as required, depending upon the client's target.

Level One

In level one, the patient is usually miserable and have lost control over themselves: they may be attempting to harm themselves, using drugs, or involving themselves in other self-destructive activities. When such clients start DBT, they may compare their experience as equivalent to "being in hell."

The main goal of this stage is to help move the client from a state of no control to the one where they learn how to get a hold of themselves.

Level Two

During level two, clients often feel like their lives are filled with desperation. They have a control on their harmful behaviors, but they still suffer, mostly due to invalidation or past trauma. This often continues to an extent that disturbs the emotional experience in such people.

The main goal of level two is to assist such people to get out of their state of desperation in order to reinstate the emotional experience. The treatment for people suffering from post-traumatic stress disorder (PTSD) falls into this level.

Level Three

In this level, the aim is to motivate the patients to live, find happiness and peace, and build self-respect. The therapist enables the client to live a normal life with moments of both happiness and sadness.

Level Four

For some clients, an additional fourth level is required in order to familiarize them with the concept of spiritual existence. This stage has been posited for clients whose life of happiness and sadness does not help them find peace or feel connected to the world.

The main goal of this stage is to assist the client move on from a feeling of incompleteness to a life which grants the clients a capacity to enjoy the feeling of freedom and joy.

What makes DBT Different?

The world is convinced that DBT can do wonders, but why is it that it continues to work even when gold standard treatments like CBT have failed?

In simple words, DBT tends to fill in the gaps left by most of the therapies including CBT. For example, CBT emphasizes changing the behaviors and thoughts of the targeted people to an extent that the clients are appalled. Most of the therapies targeting problems like stress, anxiety, PTSD, etc. do not encourage or support their clients to accept where they are right now. They are invalidating to the majority of people who consider concepts such as cognitive distortions to justify their feelings as wrong. That's where DBT differs.

DBT Promotes Acceptance-based Behaviors

Dialectical Behavior therapy is a form of CBT but what makes it more successful and unique is its special emphasis on dialectical thinking and mindfulness. Instead of treating the symptoms as problems to be solved, this therapy puts equally focuses on acceptance of experiences by incorporating acceptance-based behaviors.

It emphasizes on dialectical thinking: dialectical means a philosophical stance in which two truths or ideas, which seemingly oppose each other, exist at the same time. For example, a person coming for help may need to accept where they are right now as well as require motivation to change.

In simpler words, while DBT helps people promote the feelings of acceptance, it makes them acknowledge that they have the capacity to bring out more positivity and do much better. This is something that can exclusively be achieved by DBT.

DBT Works with Emotions

DBT is an in-depth therapy that involves a process of learning cognitive and emotional skills and applying these skills to your life. It helps tackle distressing and difficult emotions and helps you improve the capacity for emotional regulation. By improving your emotional regulation, you are able to control and express your emotions in a much better way.

DBT Enhances Capabilities with Skills Training

What makes DBT different than other approaches is that it focuses on improving the capabilities of clients by teaching them different behavioral skills. Skill training is taught in group forms in a classroom setup. A group leader is assigned to every class whose primary responsibility is to teach different skills through classroom activities, lectures, and take home assignments.

This homework helps the client to pick up the skills they learn in class and to apply them to their daily life experiences. The groups meet every week for about 2.5 hours to discuss the happenings in their daily lives. In order to grasp the full curriculum, an average person requires 24 weeks. Sometimes, the program may get repeated to form a 1-year program.

Skill Training in DBT revolves around four different modules each of which helps the client get stable in their lives. These modules include:

Mindfulness: It refers to the skill which helps you be aware and present in the current moment.

Distress Tolerance: It refers to the skill which helps you tolerate pain in tough conditions instead of changing it.

Interpersonal Effectiveness: It refers to the skill of asking for whatever you need and learning to say no without compromising on your self-respect and relationships.

Emotional Regulation: It refers to the skill of changing emotions that you wish to change.

But how does acquiring these skills help people?

Problematic behaviors occur as a way to manage a situation or resolve a difficult problem. While such behaviors provide a temporary solution or relief on a short-term basis, they are rarely effective in the long run. DBT acknowledges this and assumes that the patients are doing everything in their capacity but at the same time, they need to acquire new behavioral patterns in relevant contexts.

DBT helps such clients develop behavioral skills in the following four areas: emotional regulation, distress tolerance, mindfulness, and interpersonal effectiveness. These skills help clients acquire useful ways to navigate situations occurring in everyday life and to tackle challenges.

DBT Enhances Motivation through Individual Therapy

DBT is an individual therapy that is focused on improving the client's motivation and help them apply their learned skills to tackle specific events and functions in their lives. It is a unique approach that helps them accept their flaws yet motivates them to get up and do better instead of treating clients like victims that need sympathy.

DBT Ensures Generalization

DBT includes telephone coaching and other ways of coaching to provide their clients with in-the-moment support. The goal is to coach them on how to use DBT skills to cope with a hard situation arising at any point in their lives.

Therapists are available all the time to guide you through a difficult situation which is something that seldom occurs in other therapy sessions.

DBT Structures the Environment via Case Management

DBT incorporates case management strategies that help the client manage their own life including social and physical environments. The therapists apply the same validation, problem-solving, and dialectical strategies to enable the client to analyze their problems without any external help. This empowers them to manage their problems on their own with minimal interference by therapist unless when it becomes absolutely necessary.

DBT: A Recap

In short, Dialectical behavior therapy or DBT is a form of behavioral therapy introduced by Dr. Marsha Lineham, an American psychologist who found CBT as a therapy inefficient to help people with suicidal tendencies. The foundation of this therapy utilizes the basic concepts of the standard CBT but with additional adaptations to meet the particular needs of people experiencing intense emotions.

The basic aim of DBT is to empower you to manage difficult emotions by experiencing, recognizing, and accepting them. As you learn how to accept and control our emotions, you are better able to get over the harmful behaviors. To attain this goal, DBT therapists utilize a balance of change and acceptance techniques, something that is missing in other therapies meant for treating behavioral problems.

In DBT, therapists help you find the perfect balance between acceptance and change via four different elements: [5]

- Skills training (in groups)
- Individual therapy
- Telephonic coaching
- Consultation group of therapists

A typical course of DBT includes homework and take home assignments which usually continues for approximately a year. A lot of people may find it quite hard to develop DBT skills in the beginning because it includes accepting your flaws while working hard to change them. However, with the passage of time, you will come to realize that all your efforts were worthwhile.

Summary

If you are living with an anxiety disorder, you most likely acknowledge that feeling in control of yourself is a validating, valuable feeling. DBT can help you achieve this feeling though group skills training, trained therapists, and skills coaching. All these parts will work together to make sure that DBT offers you skills that you can put into practice to help you get a full control over how you feel and live.

DBT is currently operating on four different levels- Mindfulness, Interpersonal Effectiveness, Distress Tolerance, and Emotional Regulation- to help people get over their worst fears and depressive states. The next sections will highlight how four of these components can help you achieve stability in life.

DBT Distress Tolerance and Mindfulness Skills

Now that the concept of DBT is clear, let's move on to discuss the first two components of DBT- Mindfulness and Distress Tolerance and their role in the treatment of behavioral disorders

What are DBT Mindfulness Skills?

Mindfulness refers to paying attention to what is happening at the moment "on purpose." When you are practicing mindfulness, you are focusing your attention on the present experience, noticing whatever is happening at the exact moment, not lost in past or wondering about the future.

Mindfulness is actually something entirely opposite to being on automatic pilot. While you are on automatic pilot, you are either doing things out of habit or by rote. For example, many people relate to a condition where they arrive at work but do not really remember the car ride that took you there. That is because you did not have to think about opening the car door, sitting down, putting the key in the ignition, etc. You just did all these things automatically and found yourself at your office minutes later.

Doing things in an autopilot mode is not bad. It is actually quite useful in a way that it helps save energy and time. Problems begin to arise when you start living most of your life in this mode instead of actually being present in the moment.

Why does Mindfulness Matter?

Mindfulness is like a magic ingredient that helps you control your sentiments and take a step back from intense emotions. When you take a step back and notice what is happening, you are less likely to experience in out-of-control emotions.

"Mindfulness is powerful"

When you use mindfulness to control your attention, you open yourself to a whole new world of choice. You do not need to act and react out of fear, habit, or intense emotions.

The benefits of mindfulness have been well-researched, especially during the last few years. A regular practice of mindfulness has been shown to decrease distraction, increase emotional regulation, improve anger management, and decrease depression.

Mindfulness in DBT

Mindfulness forms the backbone of DBT. It is, in fact, the first skill taught to the patients opting for DBT. This is because, without mindfulness, it is not possible to alter long-standing patterns of acting, thinking, and feeling.

"Mindfulness is the core skill underlying all other skill sets in DBT"

It is central to getting through difficult situations, resolving interpersonal conflicts, and regulating emotions.
Mindfulness is also a primary component for accessing your Wise Mind, an important foundational concept in DBT. Wise Mind is said to be the synthesis of a Reasonable Mind and an Emotion Mind. Once you find your Wise Mind, it gets easier to know what's real for you and act according to it.

The concept of mindfulness in DBT revolves around two questions: "what to do" and "how to do it." These are known as the "What" and "How" skills.

The 'What' Skills

There are three skills that comprise the "What" of mindfulness: [6]

1. Observe
2. Describe
3. Participate

The Observe Skill

Observe means noticing any direct sensory experience. It is what you fee, see, taste, sense, hear and touch without judging it, labeling it or reacting to it. This is a bit tricky for most of the people at first; your mind wants to label what is happening around you instead of just being with the sensations of an experience. While you practice the Observe skills, you are permitting your immediate experience to happen without trying to change it or pushing it away.

Like all the skills, Observe skill is experiential. This indicates that the intellectual understanding of this skill is not sufficient; you have to experience it for yourself to truly understand it. For example, listening to the sounds around you, just noticing them without passing any comments, is an example of observing skill of mindfulness in DBT.

The Describe Skill

The Describe skills build on the Observe skill. While Observe is only bare-bones attention-noticing something without adding a label or a story-Describe includes putting the observed experience into words, whether it is an emotion, thought, or a sensation.

Sounds like a piece of cake, right? Not quite.

The tricky part is that DBT mindfulness demands you to practice the Describe skill by sticking to the facts and refraining from any personal assumptions or interpretations. So when you Describe an experience, you label thoughts as thoughts, feelings as feelings, and emotions as emotions only without adding any labels, judgments, concepts, and opinions.

The Describe skill is an excellent tool to help you NOT mistake every thought or feeling of yours for a fact. For example, just because you are feeling unlovable doesn't justify it as the truth. The Describe skill is also a great tool for reducing reactivity, especially in emotionally sensitive people. It does not let you jump to conclusions without checking the facts hence, saves you from a lot of trouble.

The Participate Skill

In DBT, Participate means exactly what it sounds like: it means throwing yourself entirely into an activity and letting go of judgments, fear, and self-conscious instead of sitting aside and watching. Most of the young children exhibit this skill, immersing themselves in play without any sort of inhibition.

For example, you can practice this mindfulness skill during everyday activities, for example, washing dishes. Instead of thinking about how much you hate it or planning what you will do once you are finished, you immerse yourself completely in the ongoing activity of washing dishes.

The 'How' Skills

The purpose of 'How' skills in DBT is to understand how to accomplish the 'What' skills.[7http://www.dbtselfhelp.com/html/dbt_skills_list.html] So you are supposed to practice the three What skills:

One-mindfully

This means giving your full presence in the current situation, not lost in the thoughts of the past or future. It means concentrating on one task at a time while focusing on it completely instead of splitting it between things, for example: having a conversation on the phone while cooking a meal.

Practicing this skill is important. One-mindfulness in DBT helps you open up to the potential beauty hidden in small moments. It prevents you from juggling multiple tasks because multitasking can weaken your connection with the Wise Mind, therefore, affect your decision-making skills.

Non-judgmentally

It is common to notice something and release judgments instantly, either about yourself ("I am not good at this!"), others ("He is not good at this"), your experience ("This was indeed a bad idea"), or anything else. Most of the use judge habitually, automatically, and continuously.

Judging has become such as important part of our internal dialogue that we fail to notice how judgments can increase emotional pain and potentially destroy relationships. Hence, the How mindfulness skills in DBT require you do everything non-judgmentally.

Being non-judgmental prevents the emotional charge of the situation from heightening, making it easier to look for solutions.

Effectively

This skill involves acting effectively i.e. doing what works vs. sitting aside and wishing things were different. In DBT, effectively is all about shifting your focus away from the concepts of what's fair and unfair, or who is right or wrong, and focusing on what really works.

When you are not concentrated on doing what is effective, you may act in ways that are more about proving a point or being right. Trying to be right gets in the way of getting what you need or want.

DBT Mindfulness Skills- A Case Example

If you catch yourself critically judging yourself and your actions, mindfulness can help recognize these judgemental thoughts and help discriminate them the reality i.e. what is actually happening in real time.

Let's have a look at an example.

Imagine you get to work late one day and instantly start judging yourself harshly. It might be common for you think:

- "I am such a big loser"

- "There isn't one thing I can do right"

- "What is wrong with me?"

Thoughts like these can force you to judge yourself harshly. However, it is also a classic mistake to start deeming these thoughts as true and use them to evaluate who you actually are. Thinking harshly about yourself and passing judgemental comments can negatively impact your feelings and behavior.

For instance, if you are convinced that you actually are a loser who always tries his best to do the things the right way but fails, you may end up feeling ashamed. You will start avoiding people and never take risks like speaking up in front of others. You will even forsee any brilliant thing you accomplish as the feeling of being 'useless' overshadows everything else.

Mindfulness encourages you to step aside and take out some time to evaluate what is it that's happening: you are having judgmental thoughts. But you are not defined by these thoughts. With mindfulness, you can label them as just thoughts. As you start practicing mindfulness, these thoughts start losing their impact on your mind and body. In simpler words, these judgemental thoughts are no longer 'facts.' Mindfulness also helps open up the possibility to think about a situation differently.

If you are able to take note of your self-judgments and can successfully label them as "just thoughts", this lets you access your Wise Mind which might say, "it is okay to be late for work once in a while. Everybody can get late, it is not the end of the world." It may even help you figure out different ways to avoid getting into such a situation ever again.

What are DBT Distress Tolerance Skills?

Distress tolerance skills module of DBT acknowledges the higher tendencies in certain individuals to exhibit negative behaviors. It recognizes that for such people, these behaviors may be overwhelming, therefore, they need to be addressed at once.[8] It is common for such people to become overwhelmed even when the slightest amount of stress arises, and they often end up developing negative behaviors. To help these people, most of the conventional treatment approaches emphasize avoiding painful situations. However, in the distress intolerance module, the aim is to make the clients acknowledge that sometimes, it is impossible to avoid pain and the best way to tackle such situation is to accept the things as they are and practice tolerating the pain associated with them.

The concept of radical acceptance forms the foundation of the distress tolerance module. This means succumbing to the reality of a stressful moment and acknowledging that there is nothing you can do to change it. By practicing the concept of radical acceptance without fighting the reality or being judgmental, the clients become less vulnerable to developing prolonged and high-intense negative feelings.

The distress tolerance module in DBT comprises of four different skills. These skills are meant to help individuals cope with difficult situations and experience distress without making it worse.

- Distracting
- Self-soothing
- Improving the moment
- Focusing on the pros and cons

Distracting

Distraction helps he client shift their focus from upsetting emotions and thoughts to neutral or more enjoyable activities. It basically deals in anything to help distract you from the distress, for example, a hobby, a quick walk in the garden, helping others, or watching a movie. These activities help clients separate themselves from a distressing situation or a troubled state of mind.

The acronym "ACCEPTS" is used to help individuals practice the skill of distraction. [9]

- **A**ctivities – Using positive activities to get over a distressing situation.
- **C**ontribute – Helping out people around you or your community.
- **C**omparisons – Comparing yourself to people who have more difficult lives than you or to your own self at your worst.

- **E**motions – making yourself feel different by provoking a sense of happiness or humor with corresponding activities.
- **P**ush away – Pushing your situation at the back of your mind for some time and replacing it with something less stressing on a temporary basis.
- **T**houghts – Trying to forget what's distressing you and diverting your mind to think about other stuff.
- **S**ensations – Doing something intense to make yourself spirited with a feeling which is different from the one that you are already going through, for example eating a spicy meal or hopping into the shower for a cold bath.

Self-Soothing

Self-soothing module is all about teaching you to respect yourself and to treat yourself kindly. It includes doing anything that helps you develop a positive image about yourself with the help of your 5 senses. For example, observing a beautiful view from the window (vision), enjoying the sounds of nature like birds chirping (hearing), lighting a scented candle (smell), enjoying a hearty meal (taste), and petting an animal (touch).

This skill entails using self-managed tools to calm clients when they are irritable and stressed. Learning to self-soothe is a significant milestone in distress tolerance module of DBT. When you self-soothe, you treat yourself with care, kindness, and compassion. This helps you build resilience and makes it easier to bounce back from difficult situations.

Improving the Moment

In this skill, the basic aim revolves around utilizing positive mental forces for improving your current image in your own eyes. This skill can be practiced by keeping in mind the acronym IMPROVE.

Imagery – This includes visualizing anything that relaxes in order to melt away the negative thoughts.

Meaning – This includes deriving meaning or a purpose from pain or a difficult situation. In simple words, it is all about finding a silver lining in everything you do. This helps the client find positivity in every situation and help them learn something.

Prayer – This includes praying to God in order to gain strength and confidence. Prayer tends to strengthen the spiritual side in many clients and help them pacify themselves.

Relaxation – This includes calming down your physical body and tensed muscles by encouraging relaxing activities such as listening to music, drinking warm milk, or getting a massage.

One thing in the moment – This includes encouraging the individual to be mindful and focused on a neutral activity going on in the present.

Vacation – This includes encouraging clients to take a mental break from a difficult situation by imagining something pleasant or doing something that makes them happy. It can be anything, for example, taking a trip or simply ignoring all phone calls for some time.

Encouragement – This includes making a conversation with yourself in a supportive and positive manner in order to get through a tough moment.

The IMPROVE skill helps client tolerate frustration or distress without making it worse, and in ideal conditions, aims to improve it. It is particularly for people stuck in situations which are hopeless and out of their control. Such people are unable to do anything about these critical situations and hence, feel hopeless, hurt, and depressed. For many people, such a situation may feel like a constant crisis, so the use of IMPROVE skill helps them get through this situation and regain confidence.

Skill No. 4: Focusing on Pros and Cons

In this particular skill, you are usually asked to make a list of all the pros of the tolerating a stressful events and compare it with the cons if you do not tolerate it (i.e. coping with it through self-destructive behaviors). The main idea of this is to help them remember now avoiding to confront a difficult situation in the past has affected them in a negative way and to make them realize how it will feel to be able to tolerate the current stress without acquiring negative behaviors. This helps the patients reduce impulsive reactions.

Summary

The distress tolerance skills taught as a part of DBT mainly focus on dealing with suffering and pain that is inevitable to the human conditions. The distress tolerance module provides the clients with beneficial tools to help them maintain their senses and balance in critical conditions. It teaches them to accept distress and manage it using healthier ways instead of acquiring negative behaviors. Following it supports the clients to learn how to authentically connect with other people, be open to your emotions, and respond flexibly to the ups and downs of life.

By practicing how to distract themselves, improve their current moments, self-soothe their mind and body, and balance the pros and cons of a particular situation, the clients are able to weather any distressing moment and reduce the destructive impulses and painful feelings. It will help them take a break and return to life in a calmer, rejuvenated, and a more focused state, like a, filled up gas tank which can now go on for miles.

DBT Interpersonal Effectiveness and Emotion Regulation Skills

We all tend to go through millions of emotions on a daily basis. These emotions not only affect our own state of mind but also govern out interpersonal relationships which, in turn, define our personal and social lives. Dialectical Behavior Therapy acknowledges the importance of emotional regulation and interpersonal relationships and comprises two separate modules to address the problems related to these aspects. [10]

What are DBT Emotion Regulation Skills?

Emotion regulation forms an important module of the dialectical behavior therapy with the purpose of teaching the clients all necessary skills to get a hold of themselves in negative situations and focusing on increasing the positive experiences. Emotional regulation refers to a complex combination of ways through which a person can relate to and act on his/her emotional experiences. This generally includes the potential of understanding and accepting the emotional experiences, the ability to rely on healthy strategies to manage uncomfortable emotions whenever it is necessary, and the skill of observing appropriate behaviors in a stressful state of mind. [11]

"Control your emotions or be controlled by them"

It is common for clients with high emotional sensitivity to get stuck in a vicious cycle of negativity often initiated by negative circumstances. These thoughts prompt an individual to respond by developing adverse or heightened emotions, eventually leading to the development of harsh choices and self-destructive behaviors. More negative emotions, such as self-loathing or shame, may follow this detrimental behavior. For such clients, emotion regulation in DBT may be of significant help.

People who have a good control of their emotion regulation are better able to control the urges to engage in impulsive behaviors like self-harm, physical aggression, or reckless behaviors during the time of emotional stress.

The DBT emotional regulation module comprises of 3 goals:
1. To develop a better understanding of your emotions
2. To decrease emotional vulnerability

3. To reduce emotional suffering

A significant feature of DBT emotion regulation is making yourself understand that it is not bad to suffer from negative emotions. They are not something that you must struggle to avoid at all costs. You must make yourself realize that negative emotions are part of your normal life and will occur no matter how hard you try. At the same time, there are different ways of accepting these emotions and allowing yourself to forgo them so that you do not remain under their control.

1. Understanding Emotions and Naming them

This skill involves recognizing emotions and labeling them. Clients are familiarized with the concept of descriptive labelling. They are then taught to use labels such as "anxious" or "frustrated" instead of general terms like "feeling bad." This is because vaguely defined emotions and much harder to manage. Another important aim of this skill is to teach the client the difference between primary and secondary emotions.

A primary emotion refers to your first response to any moment or triggers in the environment surrounding you. On the other hand, a secondary emotion refers to a response directed towards your own thoughts, for example, feeling sad about letting your anger out. These emotions are usually destructive and increase your likelihood of developing destructive behaviors. So, it is important to not only label your primary and secondary emotions but to also accept your primary emotion without judging yourself for having to deal with it in the first place.

In a normal DBT skill session, group leaders tend to discuss the myths relating to emotions that have plagued our society, for example, the common misinterpretation that there are certain "right" or "wrong" ways to feel in particular situations. An additional topic is to explain the primary purpose of emotions- which is to alert you that something around you is either problematic or beneficial. These emotional responses get stored in memory and help you prepare yourself to encounter similar situations in the future. In addition to this, your emotions help communicate messages to others via words, body language, and facial expressions.

2. Decreasing Emotional Vulnerability

In order to practice this skill, the suitable acronym is PLEASE MASTER. [12]

PL – indicates taking good care of your **p**hysical health and treating any illness or pain.

E – represents **e**ating a nutritious and balanced diet and shunning foods with excessive caffeine, fat, and sugar.

A – indicates **a**voiding drugs and alcohol which aggravate emotional instability and are not good for your mental health.

S – signifies getting adequate **s**leep on a daily basis.

E – involves **e**xercising every single day

MASTER – involves performing any task that builds competency and confidence every day

This component of Emotion Regulation particularly focuses on decreasing the emotional vulnerability by building positive experiences and balancing the negative feelings. For this purpose, clients are asked to plan on more experiences that bring them happiness and provide them with positivity. This may include participation in a sport or hobby, going out for coffee with a childhood friend, reading a good book, or doing any activity that provides them with individual contentment.

While doing these activities, the clients are asked to remain mindful, focusing on what they are currently doing. If a client is finding it difficult to focus their attention on the current activity, they have a choice to try out another activity. Planning future and establishing goals in the long run often brings positive experiences for most of the client. So, it is a part of this activity to plan ahead for future, for example, choosing a different career or moving to a different city.

3. Reducing Emotional Suffering

Reduction of emotional suffering is the last part of DBT Emotion Regulation which encompasses the following skills:

1. Letting go
2. Taking opposite action

Letting go means using mindfulness to have a complete awareness of your current emotional state. It further involves labeling this emotional state and forgoing it intentionally instead of avoiding it, fighting it, or dwelling on it. This may require you to take a deep breath and imagine yourself float away from the problem. Compare your emotion with a wave of water that keeps on coming and going.

Taking opposite action includes engaging in certain typical behaviors that are opposite to whatever a person is feeling at the moment. For instance, if a person is sad, they may try to be active, stand straight, and speak confidently; as a person would if they were happy. When an individual experiences anger, they may behave as If they are calm by adopting a soft tone or doing something good for someone. This skill does not aim at denying the current emotion; the client must still name the emotion and be able to let it go. However, acting the opposite is likely to lessen the duration and intensity of the negative feelings.

The DBT leaders try to make the clients learn these skills in group therapies. Sometimes, the clients are asked to get involved in role plays in order to help them use these newly learned skills in their everyday lives. Ultimately, these skills help empower people to regulate the emotions instead of being regulated by them.

What are DBT Interpersonal Effectiveness Skills?

Interpersonal effectiveness means the ability to interact with other people. It encompasses all the skills you use to:

- Attend to your relationships
- Maintain a balance between priorities and demands

- Balance out your "wants" and "shoulds"
- Develop a sense of self-respect and mastery [13]

Why are Interpersonal Effectiveness Skills Important?

DBT consider interpersonal skills as an important part of the treatment because they teach us the methods of communicating with other people. The way we communicate with others, in turn, determines the quality of our social life which has a major influence on our overall well-being, self-confidence, and self-esteem. For this reason, interpersonal effectiveness is the main focus of DBT. In fact, it is taught as the second core skill module in DBT sessions, with lots of resources and materials dedicated to improving the interpersonal skills of the clients. [14]

To enable the clients to establish communication with others, they are made to learn certain skills that help them get involved everyday chats more thoughtfully and in a deliberate manner instead of speaking impulsively due to sheer stress or distressing emotion. While there are a lot of skills associated with communication and interactions, DBT mainly focuses on two components:

1. The skill of asking for things that you need or want

2. The skill to deny requests when suitable

DBT founder Dr. Marsha Linehan has identified three different forms of effectiveness that need to be addressed in this module:

- Objective effectiveness
- Relationship effectiveness
- Self-respect effectiveness

Under any circumstances, all the above-mentioned types must be taken into account. It is also important to prioritize them according to the needs as this satisfies a person with his interactions as well as the outcomes.

'Objective effectiveness' refers to the goal or main motive behind a certain interaction that is directly linked to a tangible result. A typical example includes a woman who wishes that her husband calls her to inform her whenever he is working late. **'Relationship effectiveness'** indicates the ultimate goal of a conflict-free relationship. In the previous example, the wife may rank harmony and emotional closeness as her first and highest priority. Lastly, **'self-respect effectiveness'** can be considered as a priority in case of this woman if she starts feeling that her husband is being disrespectful to her by not calling her according to her wishes.

Dialectical behavior therapy utilizes different acronyms for helping their clients learn the skills tied to each type of effectiveness. In the case of objective effectiveness, DEAR MAN is the acronym of choice.

Describe: Describing the situation in solid terms and while avoiding any judgment.

Express: Expressing feelings and communicating them to the other party to let them know how the situation is making you feel.

Assert: Asserting your wishes and clearly stating what want or do not want.

Reinforce: Reinforcing why you desire a particular outcome and reward people responding positively to your request.

Mindful: Being mindful and investing your attention in the current moment, focusing on the task at hand.

Appear: Appearing confident, acquiring a confident tone and posture, and maintaining eye contact during conversations.

Negotiate: Being ready to get into negotiations, believing in "give and get", and acknowledging everyone involved in the negotiations possess valid feelings and needs.

For **relationship effectiveness**, the acronym used in DBT is GIVE:

Gentle: Approaching the other in a non-threatening and gentle manner, avoiding judgmental comments and attacks.

Interested: Acting interested by giving others a chance to speak and listening to them wholeheartedly, and avoiding interrupting them just to give in your own opinions or judgments.

Validate: Validating and acknowledging the wishes, opinions, and feelings of other persons

Easy: Assuming an easy manner by adopting a light-hearted tone and always bearing a smile on your face.

Lastly, the acronym used for **self-respect effectiveness** in DBT interpersonal effectiveness module is FAST:

Fair: Being fair to yourself and to others in order to avoid the development of resenting emotions on both sides.

Apologize: Apologizing less and taking the responsibility only when it is appropriate.

Stick: Sticking to your core values and not compromising your veracity to achieve a certain outcome.

Truthful: Being truthful while avoiding exaggerations or the portrayal of helplessness just to manipulate others.

Summary

The interpersonal effectiveness skills in DBT sessions can successfully increase the positivity in a person, irrespective of the ways in which clients prioritize objective, self-respect, or relationship effectiveness for a particular interaction. When used the right way, the DEAR MAN-GIVE-FAST skills can help you convey your wishes and needs clearly, without other people having to "read your mind." It makes you capable of asking for what you truly want without compromising on your integrity while considering the feelings of other person and keeping your relationship with them preserved.

Stress: The Basics

Your phone is ringing off the hook. Your cell phone is flooding with messages. You are an hour late for a deadline with your boss continuously checking on you, asking you how the project is going. You haven't been able to take your lunch properly and the pressure is killing you. You are stressed out, to say the last.

The scene sketched above signifies an act full of acute stress. It is short-term, meaning it won't last longer than a day or maybe two, and it may actually be beneficial for your health in certain ways. However, if your life starts feeling like this every single day of the week, you might be suffering from chronic stress. This type of stress is extremely dangerous to your health if you do not manage to overcome it.

What Causes it?

Stress can be defined as the normal physical response to life events that is often threatening or can disturb the balance of things in a certain way. The human body has a way of protecting itself in such times; this is what you know as the fight or flight response, or stress. [15]

Stress does not always harm you. In fact, good stress allows you to stay focused or alter sometimes. For example, the stress response in a life-threatening situation may have life-saving results. It can help you handle the challenging situation, such as completion of demanding work tasks. Nevertheless, there is also bad stress that can damage your body and deteriorate the normal functioning of the body.

A stressful situation- whether it is psychological or environmental- triggers a cascade of stress hormones leading to the production of a well-orchestrated series of physiological changes. A stressful event can make your heart pound and increase breathing rate. Your muscles tense up and beads of sweat cover your entire body.

These reactions, as a whole, constitute the fight-or-flight response, which is a means of surviving. It enables us to get through life-threatening situations without damaging ourselves. It includes a carefully planned sequence of changes in body hormones and the consequent physiological changes that can instantaneous help someone fight the potential threat or flee the situation to safety. However, your body also has a potential to unnecessarily respond to the conditions which may not be threatening your life, such as work pressure, traffic jams, and family problems.

Scientists have been struggling to learn the exact reasons why these reactions take place along with their possible mechanisms for decades. They have finally gained insights into the effects of chronic stress on the psychological and physical health. Frequently exposing the body to stress and consequently, the stress response to cope with it can hit your body in a negative way. Chronic stress has been known to cause hypertension, promote the development of cholesterol deposits that block the arteries, and trigger certain changes in the structure of brain leading to depression, anxiety, and addiction. The preliminary research also suggests that long-term stress can also lead to obesity, either directly (forcing you to eat more) or through indirect mechanisms (decreasing exercise and sleep).

Where does Stress Come from?

The stress response takes its origin in the brain. When you confront an oncoming car or sense any other danger, the ears or eyes (or sometimes both) process the information and send it to the amygdala, a part of the human brain that carries out emotional processing. The amygdala, which normally interprets the sounds and images, perceives an imminent danger, and instantly forwards a distress signal to the hypothalamus.

The hypothalamus is like the command center of the brain. It is in communication with the rest of the body via the autonomic nervous system (ANS), a system that keeps a check on all the reflexive activities going on inside the human body. These activities include every involuntary process such as breathing, dilation or constriction of vessels, and heartbeat. There are two components of the ANS, the parasympathetic nervous system (PANS), and the sympathetic nervous system (SANS).[16] The SANS is like the gas pedal of a car. It can trigger the fight-or-flight response and trigger certain biochemical reactions to release energy in order to respond to the perceived danger. PANS, on the other hand, functions as a brake. It triggers the "rest and digest" response responsible for calming down the body once the danger is gone.

As your body gets under stress, the amygdala senses the situation and generates a distress signal. This signal travels all the way to hypothalamus where it actives its sympathetic component by increasing the activity of the adrenal glands. The adrenal glands, in turn, respond by releasing epinephrine hormone into the blood. As this hormone circulates through your body, it induces certain physiological changes. The heart starts beating faster, pushing the blood into the muscles and other vital organs of your body. The blood pressure and pulse rate go up and you start breathing at a rapid rate. The airway tracts get dilated, making it possible for the lungs to breathe in oxygen in quantities much higher than the one inhaled in usual circumstances. The extra oxygen goes to the brain where it increases the level of alertness. The hearing, sight, and other senses sharpen. Epinephrine also induces the release of glucose and fat from storage sites of your body. As the nutrients enter the blood, they start circulating in the whole body, providing adequate energy to every corner.

All these changes happen as such a fast rate that people are not able to notice them. The wiring is so rapid that the hypothalamus and the amygdala start this stress cascade even before the visual centers in your brain have finished assessing the situation. This is what enables you to get out of the way of an approaching car even before your brain is able to comprehend what you are doing.

As soon as the elevated levels of epinephrine in your blood normalize, the second constituent of the stress response is initiated by your hypothalamus which includes the HPA axis. This network comprises of the hypothalamus (H), the pituitary gland (P), and the adrenal glands (A).

The HPA axis depends on a cascade of hormonal signals to press down the sympathetic nervous system. If your brain keeps perceiving a certain thing as potentially harmful, a hormone called corticotropin-releasing hormone (CRH) gets released from the hypothalamus. The receptors of CRH are located on the pituitary gland where this hormone binds to release another hormone known as adrenocorticotropic hormone (ACTH). ACTH reaches the adrenals and prompts them to release another hormone called cortisol. This revs up the body and keeps it on high alert. As soon as the threat passes, the cortisol levels decrease. This is when the parasympathetic system starts dampening the stress response.

Using DBT to Manage Stress

The Distress Tolerance Skills taught as a part of DBT can enable you to survive stressful situations without harming yourself. They may not provide you with strategies to help you in the long run but can help you learn skills sufficient to manage yourself successfully when the time gets tough. Strategies that you can apply to get through intense stress include:

Distraction

Stress can cause you to get stuck in rumination and worry. Indulging your mind and body in a task that diverts your attention and prevents you from thinking about whatever is stressing you, at least for some time, can provide you with enough time to think about the stressor and ponder over how to get through it. Call a friend, work out, read your favorite book, or watch a funny movie to distract your mind from the stress. [17]

Self-Soothe

Remember to be gentle and kind to yourself. It is common to be hard on yourself, especially during the times of stress. You judge your abilities and feel like you are unable to handle your problems. Incorporating soothing activities in your everyday life can help you handle the times of stress and tension. Listen to soothing music, bake cookies, watch a beautiful sunset, or eat your favorite food to soothe your body.

Try Relaxing

Following the distress tolerance module requires you to practice relaxation, for both the mind and the body. Try all the activities that will calm you. Take part in relaxation exercises or go for a hot shower. Avoid performing multiple tasks at the same time and try focusing on the currentt activity only. Form a soothing image in your mind.

Ponder on the Pros and Cons

Take a paper and pen and make two lists stating the advantages as well as the disadvantages of a stressful situation. Pen down how stress can damage you if you do not care about it. Think of all the ways in which stress will help you evolve and grow as a person. Once you are done, go through the lists once again to motivate yourself.

Breathe

Observe your breathing pattern a little more closely. Try deep breathing or count your breaths to increase the focus of your mind. This can help you calm down and be more attentive.

Summary

These days, it is quite easy to fall into a rabbit hole and lose the most important things in your life, all thanks to consistent stress. Keep in mind that in any moment of distress, you have the control, even if this means letting go of things over which you have no influence. It may not be practically possible for you to solve every single problem in your life, but with DBT distress tolerance skills, you can definitely manage your frustrations much more confidently.

Do not let stress get the best of you!

Worry: Self-help Approaches

Worry- a natural constituent of the human condition, has played a vital role in the survival of mankind. It helps you cope with the many challenges you face on a daily basis. At the same time, worry that is too frequent, too unrelenting, and too intense can cut down on the element of joy and happiness.

What Causes it?

We all feel worried. We are well aware of that feeling that something is wrong and how it keeps nagging us. We are also familiar with the persistent anxiety that it creates. But what exactly is worry and where does it come from?

Worry took its origin from *wyrgan- a* word belonging to the Old English vocabulary which means 'to strangle.' During the 16th century, worry took on the meaning 'to assault verbally.' In the 17th century, it was used to describe something that 'bothers, persecutes, or distresses. Today, the modern definitions describe worry as "to cause someone to feel anxious or distressed" or "to feel uneasy and troubled."

Worrying is not a pleasant emotion but is definitely an essential emotion hard-wired into the humans to help them survive. We worry about a certain thing because we perceive it as an imminent threat to our existence. Worry causes us to focus on this threat and protect ourselves from its wrath. In the prehistoric days when the concept of worry did not exist, the carefree cave people were often eaten by wild animals or killed by hostile tribes because they did not worry about the potential threats or did not focus on them. Those who did worry survived and passed their genes to the next generations. In short, worry has been keeping humans alive as a species since the dawn of mankind. [18]

Let's be honest, real dangers to our wellbeing, health, and livelihoods certainly exist. You want to keep yourself aware of these threats and take precautionary steps to protect yourself. You want to be extra careful against these threats which can hit you in the form of injury, accidents, or illness. In simpler words, a certain form of worrying carries an adaptive value the goal of which is to identify and get rid of these threats and protect yourself from these unnecessary dangers.

Unfortunately, worry can also morph from the practical, healthy form of vigilance and concern to a preoccupation with the perception of incredibly unlikely threats or threats that are not particularly damaging. Such worries may make you obsessed on this low-consequence, low-probability occurrences to such as extent that they start damaging your life. It is these worries which can, going back to the Old English meaning, metaphorically strangle you.

Unhealthy worry refers to a complex emotion involving negative thinking, fear, and physical anxiety. It is a concept which is not easy to wrap your arms around. While it indicates other problems in life, the worry is a problem in itself. Unhealthy worry develops from the emotional baggage that you acquire as a child which makes you believe that that you are not capable of protecting yourself in dangerous situations.

Using DBT Skills to Manage Worry

There is no overnight solution to manage worry but there is one that actually works: DBT. The troubling thoughts might linger for a very long time, but you can easily develop a Teflon mind. It only requires a bit of an effort.

Look for the Canaries in the Coal Mine

Recognize that the thoughts that are worrying you are just thoughts. It may take time to develop this skill but you can adopt it relatively quickly. It is the negative emotions that are trickier to handle. These two may gang up to you; negative thoughts leading to negative emotions and vice vera; trapping you in a loop of awfulness.

When you get lost in worrying thoughts, you tend to forget your body. What you need to do is start noticing the physical sensations accompanying your emotions. Sweating. Shallow breaths. Muscle tightening. Whatever you do worry starts bothering you.

Get a paper and a pen and start making a list. Recall every little thought that crosses your mind when you are worried. Note down any physical manifestation that comes by during a stressful event. This is what you call finding canaries in the coal mine. Notice what actions are you driven to take when you are worried (such as procrastination, alcohol, playing video games, etc.). Familiarize yourself with the list so that the next time worry strikes, you know what you are dealing with.

Avoid Avoiding

> *"David Barlow, an expert in the treatment of anxiety disorders, says that one of the most important things people suffering from an anxiety disorder can do is to stop avoiding their emotion." (Barlow, Allen, and Choate)*

Why? Because you need to prove that your worries are wrong. If you keep avoiding triggers, it is just going to keep the anxieties alive. When you worry and then realize that your concern was silly, this produces a phenomenon called "extinction", and the worry eventually stops.

On the other hand, persistently avoiding what you feel makes you believe these things are real and that fearing them is the right thing to do. This is what you call 'reinforcement' and it only strengthens the worry.

Whenever your mind signals you to avoid a certain situation, recall that this is wrong. Allow yourself to appreciate the moment by considering it as a chance to fight your fear and get away from your worries. So you have to shift your focus away from the disturbing thoughts back to the concrete world.

Now that you know about the most important thing NOT to do, let's move on to the one that you should be doing.

Identify

Do you ever look back at a moment or worry and think, "wow it really freaked me out"?

This is because you failed to realize this at the moment. Worries tend to sneak up on you, and as you undergo cognitive fusion, they overtake you. This urges you to go and make bad decisions. The best way to bypass this problem and all the fuss it creates is by identifying the increasing anxiety before it gets too late.

By now, you must have made your own list of canaries. Great. Now what you should do is start recognizing these as soon as they happen. The sooner you identify these thoughts, the action impulses, and the accompanying physical manifestations, the faster you are able to quell them.

It gets easy to identify your problem once you understand what is it that you must look for. This enables you to control it or cope with it, at least.

Engage

Have you ever found yourself swamped in troubling thoughts about a certain problem and then a bigger problem strikes you? This newly emerged problem forces you to forget about your past tensions and use whatever energy you have left in worrying about it. Notice how you are able to shift your attention. Doing it on purpose is, however, the tricky part.

The aim of this skill is to help you develop a connection with your feelings and experiences. It will help you learn how to remain in the present moment and establish a better connection with your life instead of wasting your energy in troubling thoughts. So whenever you get stuck in a stressful or worrying situation, remember to focus only on the problem at hand while avoiding any worrying thoughts which may distract you.

Channel all your attention into living the current experience. If the worry is making you distracted, remember this point, and think only about the actual problem and make efforts to deal with it only.

Tend to Your Emotions

The first thing to do in order to tend to your emotions is to learn how to identify worry. Once you have recognized yourself stuck in troubling circumstances, observe your body closely. Look for any signs related to your heightened emotions. You may notice your heart pounding, your muscles tense up, or your stomach sinking. Whatever you feel, pay close attention to it.

It is possible for your mind to divert its attention to any other topic. You may also feel like drowning in the pool of worries which diverts your attention far away from the actual problem. As soon as you find yourself in this situation, get yourself together. Try diverting all of your attention back to your body and focus on the actual problem. Do not get involved in the troublesome thoughts. Just notice them and keep returning your mind back to your body over and over again. Label your emotions, whether it is fear, anxiety, irritation, sadness, or shame. Remind yourself that it is normal to feel what you are feeling right now, that your emotion is not going to kill you.

In short, investigate, accept, and label. The worrisome feelings will eventually dissipate. It is a skill and it takes time. But it definitely works. Once you get food at it, it will be your superpower against worry.

Use Opposite Action

This may seem like advanced Kung Fu, so take it slow. In the end, this skill is what's going to prevent you from being a chronically worried individual to being a person who seldom worries. It is a mild form of "exposure therapy" and revolves around the concept of "facing your fears."

Opposite action helps your brain figure out which of the people and places are not dangerous hence, do not need to be avoided. Once your brain is able to establish this connection, your fears start diminishing. You stop avoiding people or things and gain more freedom in life to do whatever you want and go wherever you like.

Summary

Take out a moment and answer the following questions:

- Do you worry about things that do not pose a real or immediate threat?
- Do you worry so much that it becomes difficult to enjoy things?
- Are you more likely to be unhappy than happy?
- Are you not willing to take reasonable risks?
- Does worry interfere with your day-to-day activities?

If you answer no to the questions asked above, you are likely a healthy person. So keep doing whatever you are doing because you are only sensitive to real threats. You would take every reasonable step to live a happy life.

However, if the answer to most of the above questions is no, you are suffering from worry. It is necessary to take the steps mentioned above to relieve the unnecessary burden off your shoulders and start living.

Unfortunately, there is no magic pill that is going to relieve you or your worries overnight. Following DBT in a stepwise approach as mentioned above can, however, significantly impact your life and make it easy for you.

Post-traumatic Stress Disorder: Recalling and Recovering

Years after experiencing a traumatic event, you may think that your body and mind have healed; you have moved on. You think it is behind you but the memories still haunt you and the symptoms of post-traumatic stress disorder (PTSD) keep popping up every few months.

Unlike a broken arm or a rash, identifying PTSD can be quite a challenge, especially when it is happening inside your head. It may feel like rage or depression, but remember that PTSD is different from either of these problems. It latches on to everything, from your relationship at work to the way you sleep.

Identifying Post-Traumatic Stress Disorder

PTSD refers to a disorder that occurs in people who have had a traumatic past.

It is quite natural to feel afraid during or after a traumatizing situation. Fear has the ability to trigger a lot of split-second changes to prep your body against an imminent danger. This "fight-or-flight" response is what protects you from harm. Nearly every person experiences a cycle of reactions following a traumatic event, yet the majority recover from the symptoms with the passage of time. Someone who fails to recover from these symptoms and continue experiencing them even after a sufficient amount of time may be suffering from PTSD. People diagnosed with PTSD often feel frightened or stressed despite the fact that there is no danger surrounding them.

Not every person with a traumatic past develops PTSD, and not everyone suffering from PTSD shares a traumatic past. Certain circumstances, like a sudden death of someone close to you, can also trigger PTSD. The symptom can manifest themselves as early as 16 weeks following the incident. In some cases, it may take a year for these symptoms to develop. For someone to be diagnosed as a patient of PTSD, the symptoms need to be present for at least 4 weeks continuously. The severity of the symptoms must be high enough to interfere with work or relationships. The course of this illness tends to vary. Most of the individuals recover after 24 weeks following the incident while others keep struggling with it for a much longer time. In some people, the disease might become chronic. [19]

PTSD can be diagnosed by a doctor who handles the patients with mental illnesses, such as a psychologist or a psychiatrist. The following criteria need to be met for at least one month in order to confirm a case of PTSD:

- A minimum of one symptom of avoidance
- A minimum of two symptoms of reactivity and arousal
- A minimum of one re-experiencing symptom
- A minimum of two mood and cognition symptoms

Re-experiencing Symptoms

The re-experiencing symptoms commonly include:

- Bad dreams
- Flashbacks, keeping you stuck in the painful event
- The appearance of physical manifestations such as sweating and a racing heart
- Frightening notions and thoughts

Reliving the PTSD symptoms over and over again may trigger tensions in everyday life. Any object, situation, or combination of words that remind people of their traumatic past can easily trigger re-experiencing symptoms.

Avoidance Symptoms

Avoidance symptoms include:

- Trying to avoid objects, events, and places that somehow link your thoughts back to the painful event
- Avoiding any feelings or thoughts associated with the painful event

Things that remind you of your traumatic event can usually set in motion a cycle of avoidance symptoms. These symptoms force you to change your routine. Consider the example of a man who has been in an automobile accident. The man who usually prefers driving on his own might feel scared driving ever again so, he will naturally prefer to avoid it, or sometimes, even stop sitting in a car ever again.

Arousal and Reactivity

The most common arousal and reactivity symptoms include:

- Being easily frightened
- Always feeling "on edge"
- Trouble falling asleep
- Frequently suffering from angry outbursts

Arousal symptoms tend to be constant. They are not usually triggered by things that remind you of a traumatic incident. These symptoms make you feel angry and stressed. Sometimes, they even make it hard for you to perform everyday tasks such as eating, sleeping, or concentrating.

Cognition and Mood

The most common mood and cognition symptoms related to PTSD include:

- Having negative thoughts about yourself or the world
- Trouble remembering the main points of the traumatic incident
- Having distorted feelings like blame or guilt
- Losing attention to leisure activities

Cognition and mood symptoms may start or get worse after a traumatic incident but are not usually due to drugs or injury. They can make you loose interest in your family members and friends.

After a traumatic incident, it is usually natural to feel these symptoms. Many times, these symptoms resolve on their own after a period of few weeks or so. This is a state known as acute stress disorder or ASD.

However, when these symptoms persist even after a month, seriously disturbing the activities of life, and are not a consequence of medical illness, substance abuse, or anything else except the traumatic event, may be due to PTSD.

How does DBT help with Post-Traumatic Stress Symptoms

DBT is a powerful method of thought control which teaches you the necessary skills to deal with unpleasant thoughts and situations that lead to suffering. Through acceptance and change strategies, people suffering from PTSD can learn how to:

- Keep themselves aware of the triggers that cause negative reactivity
- Practice self-soothing activities to calm their body and soul
- Learn intolerance skills in order to deal with uncomforting feelings, situations, and thoughts

The DBT distress tolerance acronym ACCEPTS can help you manage PTSD. This skill stands for Activities, Contributing, Comparisons, Emotions, Push away, Thoughts, and Sensations. These techniques have been specially designed to manage your emotions and get over your past. [20]

Activities

Engage yourself in an activity. This can be any activity as long as it is healthy. Read a book, go for a walk, make some jam, or do the dishes. Anything that can keep you busy and your mind off the negative emotions associated with the past will help. When you are done, pick up a new activity. In this way, you can have a highly productive day without bringing back any haunting memories of the past.

Contributing

Do something kind for a person. Offering them help can relieve you of your emotional stress in a lot of ways. An act of service is also a type of activity which will keep you distracted and take your mind off the problem. In addition to this, contributing will help you feel good about yourself. You are not always required to do something big. Help someone cook dinner, bake cookies for a relative, or offer to mow your neighbor's lawn. Each of these activities will keep you from remembering your misery.

Comparisons

It is time to put your life in perspective. Was there ever a time when you faced more difficult challenges than you are facing now? Maybe not. Maybe this is actually the most intense situation and emotion that you have ever experience. In that case, compare yourself to another person. Has that person suffered more than you? Are you at home, comfortably lying in your bed after having a delicious dinner while in another part of the world someone is searching for leftover food in the trash and a place to sleep after suffering from a natural disaster?

The purpose of this exercise is not to increase distress or the emotional pain to your current condition. Instead, use it to add a new perspective to what you are currently experiencing.

Emotions

You have the capacity to invoke the opposite emotion of what you are feeling right now. Meditation for 15 minutes can help your anxiousness too. If a past trauma is making you depressed, watch a comedy movie. Adding a bit of the opposite emotion can help reduce the intensity of PTSD.

Push Away

If you feel like you are unable to deal with your past just yet, it is okay to push it away. Throw the problem out of your mind for a temporary duration. But how is this possible? By distracting yourself with other thoughts, activities, or mindfulness. You can set a time to come back and address your problems. Assure yourself that it will be addressed and stay calm in the interim.

Thoughts

Replace your anxious, negative thoughts with activities that occupy most of your mind, for example reciting the alphabets backward or enjoying a Sudoku puzzle. These distractions will help prevent self-destructive behaviors and reliving the traumatic events till the time you achieve emotional stability.

Sensation

Make use of your five senses to soothe yourself during times of stress. A self-soothing activity can be anything such as taking a warm bath with relaxing music and a lavender bath bomb, eating your favorite food, or tuning in to a good TV show. Anything appealing to your senses can help you cope with PTSD for the time being.

Summary

The dialectical behavior therapy skills can help you tolerate PTSD until the appropriate time to resolve the problem once and for all. It can control the symptoms of PTSD and allow you to focus more on the present with no fragments of the traumatic past. While ACCEPTS skills will enable you to focus on your current life, other modules of DBT such as group therapies and interpersonal effectiveness will motivate you to enjoy life at a basic level.

Panic Attacks: What it Feels Like?

Paula suffered from her first panic attack two months ago. She was in her office getting ready for an important presentation when, all of a sudden, an intense wave of fear hit her. A chill ran down her spine and before she could understand what was happening to her, the room started spinning. Paula felt like she was just about to throw up. Her body was badly shaking, her heart was literally pounding out of her chest, and she was unable to catch her breath no matter how hard she tried. She held onto her desk tightly until the episode passed, but it left her devastated.

Three weeks later, Paula found herself in the exact same situation, and since then, these attacks have been hitting her every now and then. She never knows when and where they will hit her, but she is extremely afraid of having one in public. To avoid this, she has been spending most of her time at home. She has stopped going out with friends and is afraid to ride the elevator to her office on the 12th floor because she fears that she will get trapped if she suffers from another panic attack.

What Causes Panic Attacks?

As with depression, paranoia, anxiety, and other clinical terms that you use every day, a panic attack may carry a different meaning for different people. For this reason, it is useful to decide on a working definition before going into any further detail.

A panic attack can be described as a sudden episode comprising of intense fear that may trigger severe physical reactions even though there is no apparent reason or any actual danger. Panic attacks are extremely frightening. When these attacks occur, you may feel like you are suffering from a heart attack, losing control, or even dying. While unraveling the brain chemistry that underpins panic attacks, it is important to think of these panic attacks as short spells of extreme, visceral fear. The type of fear that tends to keep you violently alive right in the face of danger.

How do You Get Panic Attacks

Amygdala is vital for your brain. It comprises of compact neuron clusters and is said to be the integrative center for motivation, emotions, and emotional behaviors in general. However, it is best known for the part it plays in aggression and fear. Panic attacks also stem from the abnormal activity going on in this cluster of nerves. In a review of studies published in 2012, scientists have successfully linked the stimulation of amygdala to the behavior analogs of panic attacks in humans. [21]

Another possible culprit for a panic attack is a section in your midbrain known as the periaqueductal gray responsible for regulating defense mechanisms such as freezing or running. Scientists used functional MRI scans to establish how this area lights up with activity as soon as an imminent threat is perceived. When your defense mechanisms start malfunctioning, this may lead to an over-exaggeration of threat, causing the development of anxiety, and in extreme cases, panic. But what makes people more prone to these attacks?

Genetic Predisposition

Panic attacks are almost always genetic. There are some people who will get panic attacks even with a slightest trigger, while others won't have them even if you paid them millions. All of us are born with certain innate tendencies. If you keep having panic attacks, this may be one of yours.

Anxious Patterns During Childhood

People who have a history of a depressing or stressful childhood are often the ones to suffer panic attacks in later stages of life. Such people fail to consider the world as their oyster-a place where they can enjoy their lives. Problems such as long-term illness, the death of a parent or a sibling, or an early exposure to issues like domestic violence or divorce of the parents may play a role in this.

In some cases, the reason is a parent exhibiting anxiety or overprotectiveness in response to their own anxiety. In other cases, the child is made to believe that it is his responsibility to make others happy and take care of them, forcing him to spend a large part of his life trying to please others.

A Reaction to Challenges Faced in Emerging Adulthood

Another reason why some people get panic attacks is due to the stressful experience they faced shortly before the onset of panic attacks. It can be anything, from feeling suffocated in a detestable job or relationship to losing a loved one. Alternatively, it is possible they had to face different changes which were not bad in themselves- such as completing school, switching to multiple jobs, getting married, having kids, moving to a different city, etc.- all of which imposed tensions to the point that they found it impossible to deal with collectively.

It is quite interesting that for the majority of people who suffer from panic attacks, the problem usually starts in their twenties or thirties- the years where they are struggling to establish a self-supporting life for themselves.

What is Common in all these Factors?

What causes a person to develop panic attacks? A genetic predisposition, early childhood trauma, and challenging changes in adult life. The factors common in all of these things is that these are not under your control. All three factors are growth and developmental events that can happen to some people and they're not something that is out of your jurisdiction.

Therefore, there is no reason to feel ashamed, apologetic, or guilty about experiencing panic attacks. They are not a consequence of living badly; or of making poor decisions; or of being cowardly or dumb.

Symptoms and Sequale

When a person experiences a panic attack, they feel like they are stuck in an escalating cycle of catastrophe that something bad is going to hit them in the very moment. Others feel like they are about to have a heart attack due to a pounding heart and continuous palpitations. A few people may feel that they are "losing control" and will end up doing something that embarrasses them in front of other people. Sometimes, they start breathing so quickly that they hyperventilate and feel like they're going to suffocate from a lack of oxygen.

The symptoms of a panic attack can be divided into two categories: emotional and physical

Psychological Symptoms

Suffering from panic attacks can badly affect the health of an individual. Besides the inexplicable anxiety and fear, some common symptoms of a panic attack include:

- Failure to relax
- Absent-mindedness
- Expecting danger
- Inability to focus
- Feelings of tension

- Getting annoyed easily

Physical Symptoms

The physical symptoms of panic attacks include the following:

- Inability to sleep
- Exhaustion
- Muscle contractions
- Shakiness
- Excessive sweating
- Nausea
- Increased heart rate
- Difficulty in breathing
- Increased blood pressure
- Chest pain

Sequale of Panic Attack

Panic attacks have an ability to disturb the normal functioning of your body. Mentioned below are the consequences of this disorder on various body systems.

Cardiovascular System

A panic attack can lead to palpitations, chest pain, and a rapid heart rate. The risk of developing high blood pressure or hypertension increases several folds. If you are already a heart patient, panic attacks can also raise the risk of coronary problems.

Digestive and System

A panic attack can also affect your digestive system. You may suffer from nausea, vomiting, diarrhea, and stomach aches. Sometimes, loss of appetite may occur leading to weight fluctuations in the long run.

A connection between anxiety disorders including panic attacks and the development of irritable bowel syndrome has also been established.

Immune System

Panic attack triggers the fight-or-flight response in your body by releasing certain hormones like adrenaline. In the short term, this causes an increase in your breathing rate and pulse so that your brain can receive more oxygen. This helps you respond better to the stressful situation. Panic attacks may also boost your immune system. When this happens occasionally, your body returns to normal functioning as soon as the attack is over.

But if you repeatedly suffer from panic attacks, your body never receives the signal to resume normal functioning. This may weaken your immune system, making you vulnerable to infections.

Respiratory System

Panic attacks usually trigger rapid, shallow breathing, if you are a patient of chronic obstructive pulmonary disease (COPD), you may even require hospitalization. Panic attacks can also make asthma worse.

Summary

A panic attack may happen anywhere, at any time. You may feel overwhelmed and terrified, even though there is no danger. You should remember that it is not something to feel guilty for. You were never in control of the factors responsible for this disorder so there is nothing that could have been done to prevent this. However, you can follow these tips to reduce the frequency of attacks:

- Exercise every day

- Get enough sleep
- Follow a regular schedule
- Avoid using stimulants like caffeine

Social Anxiety: The Fear of People

Cathy is standing in line at the grocery store waiting for her turn. All of a sudden, she feels like everyone is watching her. She knows it's not true, but she is unable to shake this extremely discomforting feeling off her head. This feeling isn't the for the first time. In fact, it happens every time she steps out of her house. She always feels like people are noticing her when she shops, judging her every step of the way.

Now that it's her turn, Cathy feels nervous talking to the girl who is checking out the groceries. She tries to pass a friendly smile, but her voice comes out rather weakly. "I am making a fool of myself," she wonders. Her anxiety and self-conscious rise to the roof.

What Cathy suffers from is social anxiety, a type of disorder that makes you lose confidence in yourself as you face the world. But what triggers it?

What Causes Social Anxiety?

If you are suffering from social anxiety disorder (SAD), it is possible that a number of different situations elicit fearful feelings. Any social situation carries the potential to trigger social fears. Some of the most common situations have been listed below.

Performances

Performances include public speaking, musical performances, and athletic competitions. People with social anxiety who fear these situations are unable to give their best. Fears related to public speaking often get in the way of career advancements.

Parties

Nothing triggers social anxiety more than a room full of strange faces. Meeting new people or going to a party where you do not have any acquaintances can be quite challenging for a person suffering from social anxiety.

Conversing with Authority Figures

Social anxiety can make it difficult for you to speak to the authoritative figures such as teachers, employers, and professors.

Making Small Talk

Small talk usually comes easily for most of the people. However, for those with social anxiety, this kind of conversation can be challenging.

Dating

Every aspect of dating triggers social anxiety, from going on first dates to making phone calls to being intimate.

Writing

Writing in front of others is a common trigger of social anxiety for most of the people. This feeling of tension stems from the fear that other people are going to see your hands shake as you write.

Giving Opinion

Do you usually refrain from stating your opinion? Do you prefer going along with what others propose even if you do not agree with them? People with social anxiety are often not confident enough to state their opinions for the fear that people may criticize them.

Reading Aloud

In addition to speaking on a public platform, some individuals also fear reading aloud in front of people due to social anxiety.

Using Public Toilets

Paruresis refers to the fear of using public toilets which is often debilitating for people with social anxiety and may trigger symptoms.

Eating in front of Others

Some victims of social anxiety fear to eat in front of others. The thought of spilling a drink of eating with shaky hands in front of the people may trigger an attack.

The Driving Factors

The following factors may play a role in the development of social anxiety:

Genetic Basis

Genetic predisposition strongly determines the possibility of social anxiety in people. Individuals whose parents suffered from this problem at some point in their lives are more likely to inherit it. However, one cannot estimate the extent to which genetics affect this link. This is important given the significance of the parenting style as a factor for social anxiety (discussed later). Since the parenting style is something that naturally gets affected due to the presence of social anxiety in parents, it is also likely to be equally responsible for passing on this problem anxiety to the children. [22]

Recent evidence has explored specific genetic markers linked with social anxiety, particularly focusing on the alterations in a gene known as SLCGA4. This gene plays a role in the transportation of a neurotransmitter named serotonin, a chemical agent that soothes your nerves and regulates mood. An excess and lack of serotonin are said to be the direct contributors to most of the symptoms of social anxiety. Social anxiety disorder (SAD) triggers the body to consistently produce serotonin without any fluctuation. [23]

Abnormalities in the SLCG4A-related activities also contribute to the development of SAD. Moreover, these faulty genes are also passed from parents to children, proving the role of genetic predisposition.

Environmental Influences

Social anxiety shares strong ties with stressful events of life and a traumatizing childhood. The following factors can predict the development of SAD to a great extent:

- Teasing or bullying by peers
- Sexual, emotional, or physical abuse
- Death of a loved one
- Desertion by the parents
- Family conflicts
- Maternal stress, particularly during infancy or pregnancy
- Domestic violence

Traumatic events can make an individual believe that this world is a scary place with a high level of unpredictability. It is can be particularly disheartening and shocking for kids to notice their caregivers portraying hurtful or selfish behaviors.

The Role of Parenting Approaches and Styles

Extensive research has etablished negative parenting appraoches as a risk factor for social anxiety. Overly concerned or overly critical parents who fail to show any affection can distort the image of the world in the eyes of the children. Growing up in such environments may even force them to become less trustful and more fearful of the world.

Their self-confidence and self-esteem take a hit as well. In such circumstances, parents fail to realize that their actions are harmful. Portrayal of negative behaviors by the parents can cause trouble for their children, especially during the later stages of life. SAD is not usually diagnosed until childhood but the symptoms start manifesting themselves in late childhood or sometimes, in early adolescence. This reinforces the association of parenting style as an important formational factor with SAD.

Consequences of Social Anxiety

Enduring social anxiety can severely limit your ability to live normally. Social anxiety is, to a certain extent, a response to a perceived negative evaluation by the people around you. The affected people always dread of being evaluated by the public while participating in a social situation. This fear of evaluation not only hinders you in your relationships and social interactions but also physically and psychologically. [24]

Physical Effects

The physical effects of social anxiety are common, even when it primarily involves social and psychological behaviors. Following is a list of physical effects that social anxiety can bring about:

- Tightness in chest
- Increased heart rate
- Shortness of breath
- Problems in occupational functioning
- Nausea
- Gastrointestinal upset
- Shakiness
- Profuse sweating
- Dizziness which may progress to faintness

- Increased muscle tension

Psychological Effects

Social anxiety involves extreme anxiety and the fear of constantly being judged by others, to the point that severe psychological problems may arise. Some of the most common psychological problems include:

- Emotional detachment
- Inferiority complex
- Low self-esteem
- Excessive self-consciousness
- Emotional dysregulation
- Panic attacks
- Severe depression
- Irrational thoughts

Social Effects

Fear of negative evaluation brought upon by social anxiety can permanently damage your social life. Some of the most common social effects related to social anxiety include:

- Avoidance of social functions or events
- Isolation from other people
- Difficulties in forming or sustaining relationships

- Inability to carry on intimate relationships
- Decreased performance at work or school
- Familial/marital conflicts due to extremely low self-esteem

Summary

Social anxiety can severely affect your ability to communicate and socialize with other people. Surveys suggest that seven percent of the adults on a global level suffers from SAD which is severely debilitating, overwhelming, and not under their control. But remember that social anxiety is not untreatable. By learning the skills of mindful meditation practiced in DBT, you can regulate your emotions and behavior. This unique approach of incorporating mindfulness skills in mainstream psychology will help you regain your confidence to face the world.

Conclusion

Before DBT, John felt like the only solution was suicide. Now that he has completed his treatment, he is able to look forward. His emotions and thoughts used to control him; now he can control them. Of course, he has his bad days, but through different DBT skills, he has learned to ride the waves of anxiety instead of letting them swallow him.

DBT- a therapy based on validation- is all about accepting the feelings that you have at any given point and working through them. It is a process that provides you with hands-on skills and tools to empower you to make the right decisions when you are overwhelmed or stuck in a distressing situation. DBT will help you validate yourself and become your own support rather than having to rely on outside sources for help and validation.

It will help you spot red flags- warning signs that will let you know that a crisis is coming- and help you take necessary action in order to minimize the strength and effect of this upcoming episode, even avoiding them after some time. DBT will teach you how to tolerate what you are experiencing and react to it in a healthy, resilient way.

Whatever it is that's bothering you- anxiety, worrying thoughts, a traumatic past, or extreme fear of evaluation- DBT can help. By following the steps described in the book, you will be able to break the co-dependency and the need for someone or something else to come save you, help you, or validate you. You will know how to be there for yourself. You will give up on the harming coping mechanisms and learn crisis survival skills.

So when things start becoming stressful or your emotions get out of control, remember that you have a toolkit to fight it. You are enough for yourself- all it takes is willpower and a bit of perseverance.

References

1. National Institute of Mental Health. (2018). Retrieved from: https://www.nimh.nih.gov/health/statistics/any-anxiety-disorder.shtml
2. National Health Service. (2016). Retrieved from: https://www.nhs.uk/conditions/generalised-anxiety-disorder/symptoms/
3. Chapman AL. Dialectical behavior therapy: current indications and unique elements. Psychiatry (Edgmont). 2006 Sep;3(9):62.
4. Little H, Tickle A, das Nair R. Process and impact of dialectical behaviour therapy: A systematic review of perceptions of clients with a diagnosis of borderline personality disorder. Psychology and Psychotherapy: Theory, Research and Practice. 2018 Sep;91(3):278-301.
5. Young, Kathleen (2010-03-11), "Mindfulness and DBT: "What skills"", Dr. Kathleen Young: Treating Trauma in Tucson
6. Lisa Dietz (2003). "DBT Skills List". Retrieved 2010-04-26.
7. ""Road To Resiliance" Article: What is resilience?". American Psychological Association.
8. Lisa Dietz (2003). "DBT Skills List". Retrieved 2010-04-26.
9. Stone, M.H. (1987) In A. Tasman, R. E. Hales, & A. J. Frances (eds.), *American Psychiatric Press review of psychiatry* (vol. 8, pp. 103–122). Washington DC: American Psychiatric Press.
10. Holmes, P.; Georgescu, S. & Liles, W. (2005). "Further delineating the applicability of acceptance and change to private responses: The

example of dialectical behavior therapy" (PDF). *The Behavior Analyst Today.* 7 (3): 301–311.
11. Nee C, Farman S. Dialectical behaviour therapy as a treatment for borderline personality disorder in prisons: Three illustrative case studies. The Journal of Forensic Psychiatry & Psychology. 2007 Jun 1;18(2):160-80.
12. *Linehan, M.M.; Tutek, D.A.; Heard, H.L.; Armstrong, H.E. (1994). "Interpersonal outcome of cognitive behavioral treatment for chronically suicidal borderline patients". American Journal of Psychiatry. 151 (12): 1771–1776. doi:10.1176/ajp.151.12.1771.*
13. *Dialectical Behavior Therapy Workbook: Practical DBT Exercises for Learning Mindfulness, Interpersonal Effectiveness, Emotion Regulation, & Distress Tolerance (New Harbinger Self-Help Workbook)* by Matthew McKay, Jeffrey C. Wood, and Jeffrey Brantley. ISBN 978-1-57224-513-6.
14. Chnag.L.K. Retrieved from: https://www.mindfulnessmuse.com/dialectical-behavior-therapy/using-d-e-a-r-m-a-n-to-get-what-you-want
15. Simandan, Dragos (2010). "On how much one can take: Relocating exploitation and exclusion within the broader framework of allostatic load theory". *Health & Place.* 16 (6): 1291–3. doi:10.1016/j.healthplace.2010.08.009. PMID 2081 3575.
16. Herbert, T. B.; Cohen, S. (1993). "Stress and immunity in humans: a meta-analytic review". *Psychosomatic Medicine.* 55 (4): 364–379. doi:10.1097/00006842-199307000-00004.
17. Greenberg. *Comprehensive Stress Management 10E.* McGraw-Hill Education. pp. 261–. ISBN 978-0-07-067104-1.

18. Borkovec TD. (2002). Clinical Psychology: Science and Practice 9, 76–80.
19. American Psychiatric Association (2013). *Diagnostic and Statistical Manual of Mental Disorders* (5th ed.). Arlington, VA: American Psychiatric Publishing. pp. 271–280. ISBN 978-0-89042-555-8.
20. "What is Dialectical Behavior Therapy (DBT)? – Behavioral Tech". *behavioraltech.org*.
21. Kim JE, Dager SR, Lyoo IK. The role of the amygdala in the pathophysiology of panic disorder: evidence from neuroimaging studies. Biology of mood & anxiety disorders. 2012 Dec;2(1):20.
22. Norrholm SD, Ressler KJ. Genetics of anxiety and trauma-related disorders. Neuroscience. 2009 Nov 24;164(1):272-87.
23. Frick A, Åhs F, Engman J, Jonasson M, Alaie I, Björkstrand J, Frans Ö, Faria V, Linnman C, Appel L, Wahlstedt K. Serotonin synthesis and reuptake in social anxiety disorder: a positron emission tomography study. JAMA psychiatry. 2015 Aug 1;72(8):794-802.
24. Watson, D.; Friend, R. (1969). "Measurement of Social-evaluative Anxiety". *Journal of Consulting and Clinical Psychology*. 33 (4): 448–57. doi:10.1037/h0027806.
25. National Collaborating Centre for Mental Health (UK. Social anxiety disorder: recognition, assessment and treatment. British Psychological Society.

Disclaimer

The information contained in **"Cognitive Behavioral Therapy & Dialectical Behavior Therapy for Anxiety -2 In 1-"** and its components, is meant to serve as a comprehensive collection of strategies that the author of this eBook has done research about. Summaries, strategies, tips and tricks are only recommendations by the author, and reading this eBook will not guarantee that one's results will exactly mirror the author's results.

The author of this Ebook has made all reasonable efforts to provide current and accurate information for the readers of this eBook. The author and its associates will not be held liable for any unintentional errors or omissions that may be found.

The material in the Ebook may include information by third parties. Third party materials comprise of opinions expressed by their owners. As such, the author of this eBook does not assume responsibility or liability for any third party material or opinions.

The publication of third party material does not constitute the author's guarantee of any information, products, services, or opinions contained within third party material. Use of third party material does not guarantee that your results will mirror our results. Publication of such third party material is simply a recommendation and expression of the author's own opinion of that material.

Whether because of the progression of the Internet, or the unforeseen changes in company policy and editorial submission guidelines, what is stated as fact at the time of this writing may become outdated or inapplicable later.

This Ebook is copyright ©2018 by **Jonathan Moran** with all rights reserved. It is illegal to redistribute, copy, or create derivative works from this Ebook whole or in parts. No parts of this report may be reproduced or retransmitted in any forms whatsoever without the written expressed and signed permission from the author.

CPSIA information can be obtained
at www.ICGtesting.com
Printed in the USA
LVHW111500160519
618103LV00001B/28/P

9 781795 206921